DIVINE
MASTERPIECE

RECLAIMING YOUR STOLEN IDENTITY & LIVING YOUR PURPOSE OUT LOUD

OBED OLIVARRÍA

metamorphosis
PUBLISHERS

OBED OLIVARRÍA

Cover design by Obed Olivarría
Typeset and inside design by Obed Olivarría

Library of Congress Control Number: 2024919150

ISBN (print edition): 979-8-9913504-0-2
ISBN (eBook edition): 979-8-9913504-1-9

First Edition: December 2024

Metamorphosis Publishers.
Santa Ana, California.

For information contact:
http://www.obedolivarria.com

CONTENTS

Preface

INTROSPECTION

"Before I formed you in the womb, I knew you; before you were born, I set you apart."

(Jeremiah 1:5)

WE ALWAYS PLAY DIFFERENT ROLES in different settings. These roles are engrained in us. For example: I am youngest brother, son, father, husband, school psychologist, musician, neighbor, etc. The list goes on for each of us. Our identity and purpose seem to change depending on our current circumstance.

But there is a problem: Christians today suffer from an identity crisis. We are not sure of who we are or what our purpose in this world is. We change from one day to the next, from one circumstance to another. But crisis always leads to introspection, and introspection always leads to the search for one's true identity.

The solution to this identity crisis is to change the way we think about ourselves. As Paul says, we must "not conform any longer to the pattern of this world, but be transformed by the renewing of our minds." (Romans 12:2)

We must ask what our identity and what our real purpose is because a stable and healthy identity allows us to take the right decisions in life. But what institutes what our identity is? Is it determined by our career choice, nationality, ethnicity, gender, or personality type? Does it even have anything to do with personal characteristics? If that is the case, then we will miss the point of why we are here on Earth, because there is no eternal purpose linked to this definition of self.

It has been proposed that we should define ourselves by what we do and by what we produce. But there is a fundamental flaw in this belief. If you are young, strong, healthy, and employed, then you might try to convince yourself that you find your identity in what you harvest or create. However, for those who do not fall into these categories, it is harder to answer the question of "who I am" because the moment that you cannot perform, you have just destroyed your own self-worth. The good news is that our identity is in who we are and Whose we are, not in what we do. On the contrary, what we do is a result of who we are.

You need to see beyond finite reality and perceive eternal existence to understand that your identity surpasses any image that we could create for ourselves. You must peer into the Divine with purpose to recognize the fact that God created you in His image to live in a relationship with Him and reflect His image. You belong to Him twice; first because He made you and formed you in His image (Genesis 1:27; Psalm 139:13), and second because He lovingly redeemed you after you had fallen (John 3:16; Romans 5:8). In this belonging, you will appreciate His love, joy, and grace. And by enjoying this relationship with your Creator, you will find a meaningful purpose and true identity as a masterpiece.

Be aware that there is a clear disparity between who the world says we are and who Christ says that we are. And it is good to know and believe everything that God says about you because if you realize who you truly are, then you will act accordingly and will experience the joy of a victorious life in Christ. You no longer need to live as a lost orphan with a misguided purpose in life.

As a child of God and as a disciple of Christ, look to Jesus to find your identity and purpose. After all, the only way to become the person God created and purposed you to be is by having a relationship with Him. Your values and perspectives in life will change as you experience the identity that is only found in Him.

It is my desire that as you embark on this journey of self-discovery, the closer you get to Jesus, the clearer your true identity and purpose becomes. May you approach it with humility and an eagerness to become who you are meant to be.

PART ONE

Identity

Chapter 1

CHRISTIAN IDENTITY THEFT

"I have been chosen by God and adopted as His child... He chose us in Him before the creation of the world to be holy and blameless in His sight. In love He predestined us to be adopted as His children through Jesus Christ... In Him we have redemption through His blood and the forgiveness of sins."
(Ephesians 1:3-8)

ONE MORE STATISTIC

MARIA GONZALEZ WAS A TWENTY-YEAR-OLD, single mother of two, from Los Angeles, and she was living life to the fullest. Let me explain. She had at least thirty-five different credit card accounts. She had charged the bill to $98,000 in electronic and furniture stores. She bought a house that cost just over $400,000 (though now it doesn't seem like much for a home, at the time that this happened, this amount was extravagant), and she splurged on a $45,000 SUV. So, no doubt, at age twenty, Maria Gonzalez was living life to the fullest.

However, there was one problem. The real Maria Gonzalez did not do any of those things. The real Maria Gonzalez was a single, full-time student in a community college. The real Maria Gonzalez purchased none of these things. She had been the victim of the crime known as "Identity Theft." It did not take long for the police to discover that a co-worker of hers had stolen her identity. When asked how she felt, the real Maria Gonzalez said, *"It was scary to know that someone else was living my life."*

One of the greatest and fastest crimes in the world is identity theft. Every year, over fifteen million Americans fall victim to identity fraud, causing financial losses totaling around fifty billion dollars. That means that almost 7% of all adults have their identities misused with each instance, resulting in around $3,500 in losses on average.

Besides that, almost one-hundred million additional American citizens have their personal identifying information placed at risk of identity theft each year when records maintained in government, health, and corporate databases become lost or stolen. Identity theft is a prevalent and expensive crime.

I want to suggest, however, that another type of identity theft is also happening right now. This is a far more dangerous and even more common crime in our society. It affects millions and millions of people every day. "Christian Identity Theft" is also taking place. Any follower of Jesus has the potential to fall victim. The problem is, however, that this identity theft, which occurs all the time, causes very little uproar.

STOLEN IDENTITY

What do I mean by Christian Identity Theft? The enemy of our existence—Satan–, is using, misusing, and abusing the identities of God's people every day. Satan seeks to rob us of the identity we have in Jesus.

He does not want us to know how interconnected we are to Jesus. He wants us to feel guilty, when we are in fact forgiven.

He wants us to feel alienated when nothing can separate us from Jesus' love. Satan wants us to forget who we are and Whose we are so that we can no longer fulfill our purpose in this world. And he has been so successful that we are not sure of who we are anymore. So, we are victims, indeed, of Christian Identity Theft.

All you must do is look at the media, watch TV, and you will see how confusing it is. Because, if you see long enough, you will think Christians are only a political action committee, and that the only thing that we do is sway votes in Congress or the Supreme Court or try to pass or deny certain bills. Or perhaps you will think Christians are only a protest movement, and that all we do is stand outside of abortion clinics and protest and yell words to make excitement and be on the evening news.

There is confusion, because if you see movies, Christians often get portrayed as wimpy and nerdy, always having problems fitting in, because apparently, they do not know how to have fun. Then other shows show Christian leaders as perverted pedophiles. Others think that we Christians always want to fight wars and try to share the Gospel with weapons and by destroying other people's cities and cultures—that is, anyone who does not look, act, or believe like us. And the saddest thing is that many times, unfortunately, they are right. But the reality is that Christian Identity Theft is happening, indeed.

JESUS' LABEL

But wait a minute! I do not know about you, but I am tired of being categorized in certain ways. I am tired of being a label! In fact, the only label that we should have is the one that Jesus, Himself, talked about, when

9

He said in John 13:45, "*By this they will know that you are My disciples, in that you love one another.*"

We, as Christians, need to put close attention to this label that Jesus gave us. That is because for so long, as a Church, we have decided that our Christian heritage be known by how well we live our lives. And, let's be honest, we have never even lived them that well. I mean, we are not getting to Heaven because of how well we live! We will be there only because faith saves us through grace. And as a Church many times we say, "*By this they shall know us ... by our enhanced hospitals, by our vigorous lifestyle, by our stand against this political movement, and by our superior education system... etcetera-etcetera... by this they shall know us.*" But, no! Jesus said, "*They will know you because of the love you have for one another!*" That is the label that Jesus, Himself, wants us to have.

I want some day for somebody to say, "*Oh! Those are the Christians! They are the ones who take care of people. They are the ones who take a homeless man and put him in a home. They are the people who know how to take a lady who is going through divorce and help her recover. They are the ones that know how to take poor people and give them an adequate education so that they can ride in the high places of life.*" I want them to know us because we know how to love! I want them to say, "*Yeah, I know those guys. They are the ones who get on your nerve, because they love you to death.*" Wouldn't you want to hear that?

Here is an eye-opener. In his quest for peace and freedom, Mahatma Gandhi, the renowned leader of the people of India, read the four Christian Gospels. Even though he was a Hindu, he had heard about Jesus and His deeds, so he wanted to learn more about Him. After reading the Gospels, Gandhi was so impressed with Jesus and what He stood for that he gave Christianity a chance. On a Sunday morning, Gandhi visited one of the many Christian churches in Kolkata. Upon reaching the entrance, however, the ushers barred his way at the door.

They told him he was not welcome there and that he could not enter this church, as it was for 'high caste' Indians and whites only. Gandhi was neither 'high caste,' nor was he of European descent. After this encounter, he rejected the Christian faith. Gandhi later declared, "I'd be a Christian if it were not for the Christians!" A British reported once asked him for more clarification on this statement, to which Gandhi replied, "I like your Christ; I just do not like your Christians. Your Christians are so unlike your Christ. If only you practiced what He preached, this world would be a better place."

Talk about a missed opportunity! And ouch! I believe Gandhi was correct in stating that we Christians miss the mark in following Jesus' footsteps. And yet, we call ourselves Christians—disciples of Jesus Christ. So we are, then, victims of Christian Identity Theft, also because of our own doing.

Now, here is the thing, though: you need to recognize who you are in Christ. If you want to live your true identity and if you want to do effective ministry in the name of Jesus, then you first need to know who you are. And in order to know who you are, you must know Whose you are. And once you know that, then you must also realize what your purpose is.

It is time to stop pretending to be something we are not. Either we are one with Christ, or we are against Him. There is no in-between. There's no middle ground. We cannot wear masks anymore. If we wear a mask for too long, we will forget who we are. And soon, we will say, "it is easier for someone else to pretend to be me than for myself to pretend to be me." But do not say that you are one with Christ if you are reluctant to identify yourself as one of His disciples in your home, in your school, in your relationships, in your social life, and wherever else you may be. Your true identity must be consistent everywhere.

TAKING THE LORD'S NAME IN VAIN

I detest identity theft! I mean, who doesn't? Good reputations and decent credit earned through years of hard work vanish because of larceny. Belongings and assets disappear because of burglary. Even God does not like it when an identity is stolen.

Now, think about this. How do you think God feels when people that claim to belong to Him misrepresent Him? How does God feel when people pretend to represent His name, yet fail to bestow His character? How do you think God felt about His misrepresentation in that church in Kolkata... and in everyday life, everywhere around the world? Don't you think that to say that you are a Christian in name only, and yet not behave like one is called to do so is another form of identity theft? How can one claim to belong to a movement of love, and go out there and live in every way, except in a way of demonstrating God's character of love? What kind of reputation does that give God when His representatives portray actions and attitudes of greed and selfishness? After all, don't these people follow the same course as the identity thieves we all detest?

I believe that to take the name "Christian" while living in un-Christ-like ways is equivalent to breaking the Third Commandment—"Thou shalt not take the name of the Lord thy God in vain." And since identity theft is theft, it also breaks the Eighth Commandment—"Thou shalt not steal." Many people think that the Third Commandment means not cursing or mentioning the name of Jesus out of context. I would like to suggest to you, however, that what is entailed in this mandate is to not pretend to carry God's last name when you live in such a way that misrepresents Him.

Think about it this way. Have you ever grabbed an apple or any other fruit that looked good, taken a bite, but then got a nasty surprise? Maybe it was rotten or sour. Maybe it was too hard or too soft. It just was not what you thought it would be. It is a horrible experience, right? What do you usually do with that fruit? You throw it away! We dislike being deceived by appearances. Well, is it possible that you are guilty of Christian Identity Theft too?

PEOPLE OF THE MASKS

Many of us live lives of contradictory principles, lives of duality with inconsistent ethical standards. Many of us say one thing and do another. Blatantly stated, we are hypocrites. Ironically, hypocrisy is one of the main reasons given by most people for either leaving the Church or for not going to church.

They usually say, "Those church people claim to be so good and holy, but in reality, they are all just the opposite. I just cannot stand being around hypocrites like that." But check out what the Bible says in response to that. Luke 6:42 reports Jesus as saying: *"How can you say to your neighbor, 'Friend, let me take out the speck that is in your eye', when you yourself do not see the log that is in your own eye? You hypocrite, first take the log out of your own eye, and then you will see clearly to take out the speck that is in your neighbor's eye."* The truth of the matter is that we are all hypocrites! We steal the identity that God, Himself, gave us!

On another passage, God accuses His people of being hypocrites. Isaiah 29:13-21 says, *"These people come near to Me with their mouth and honor Me with their lips, but their hearts are far from Me. Their worship of Me is made up only of rules taught by men. Therefore, once more I will astound these people with wonder upon wonder; the wisdom of the wise will perish, the intelligence of the intelligent will vanish. Woe to those who go to*

13

great depths to hide their plans from the LORD, who do their work in darkness and think, 'Who sees us? Who will know?'"

Jesus refers to them as "Hypocrites," which is from the same root in Greek as the word for actor, and means "one who wears a mask." Hypocrite refers to being a Greek play-actor. An actor usually wore a mask and in speech and action imitated the character of someone else while on a stage to be seen by others. The English transliteration of hypocrite has the meaning of pretending to be what one is not, especially in religion or morality. But to a certain degree, we all wear masks at various points in our lives. You might think: "Not me! I am always completely honest." And if you think that, now you are not only a hypocrite, but also a liar.

Many people are under the idea that God does not see all our lives. Let me tell you this—you can run, but you can't hide! Read Isaiah 29:15 again. It says, "Woe to those who go to great depths to hide their plans from the LORD, who do their work in darkness and think, 'Who sees us? Who will know?'"

The answer is God! God will know! He knows everything! We can pretend that because we may be good in some areas of life that there is no sin, but God sees all areas of our lives. Eventually, the truth always comes out. Jesus knows when we wear masks and pretend to be clean on the outside, when in reality we are rotten inside, just like the fruit that appears to be good but is not.

So, we all, as Christians, have lost our identity. For many of us, it has been stolen. For others of us, we have lost it or forgotten it. And many others choose to wear a mask. Where do you fit in? Are you even aware of your true identity in Christ? Do you know what you were created for?

TO SOAR THE SKY

A naturalist was visiting a farmer early one day and saw a beautiful bald eagle in the farmer's chicken coop.

"*Why in the world do you have this huge eagle living in with the chickens?*" asked the naturalist to the farmer.

"*Well,*" answered the farmer, "*I found him when he was little and raised him in there with the chickens. He doesn't know any better, and he thinks he is a chicken.*"

The naturalist was taken aback. The eagle was pecking the grain and drinking from the watering can. The eagle kept his eyes on the ground and strutted around in circles, looking every inch like a big, over-sized chicken.

"*Doesn't he ever try to spread his wings and fly out of there?*" asked the naturalist.

"*Not really. And I doubt he ever will because he doesn't know what it means to fly.*"

"*Well, let me take him out and do a few experiments with him.*"

The farmer agreed since he didn't lay eggs, anyway, and not to mention all the food he ate. But he assured the naturalist that he was wasting his time.

The naturalist lifted the bird to the top of the chicken coop fence, and said, "*Fly!*" He pushed the bird off the fence, and it fell to the ground in a pile of dusty feathers. Next, the undisturbed researcher took the messy chicken-eagle to the farmer's hayloft and spread its wings before tossing it high in the air. The frightened bird screamed and fell to the barnyard, where it resumed pecking the ground in search of its dinner.

The naturalist again picked up the eagle and gave it one more chance in a more appropriate environment, away from the examples of chicken lifestyle. He set the bird on the front seat of his pickup truck next to him and headed for the highest hill in the region.

After a lengthy climb to the top of the hill, with the bird tucked under his arm, he spoke gently to the bird, "*You were born to soar. It is better that you die here today on the rocks below than to live the rest of your life being a chicken in a barn, out of your element.*" Having said these last words, he lifted the eagle up, and once more commanded it to fly. He tossed it out in the air, and this time, much to his relief, it opened its seven-foot wingspan and flew gracefully into the sky. It slowly climbed in higher spirals, riding the wind, until it disappeared into the glare of the morning sun.

God has made you to soar in the high places of life. Do not let anyone else define your self-worth or keep you under their limiting and oppressive influence. You are a child of God with an unimaginable potential. God knows your potential, for it is He that has given you your individual missions and the gifts needed to accomplish them.

Isaiah 41:30-31 says, "*Even the youths shall faint and be weary, and the young men utterly fail; but they that wait upon the Lord shall renew their strength, they shall mount up with wings as eagles, they shall run, and not be weary, and they shall walk, and not faint.*"

Just as the eagle needed to be removed from the influence of his non-flying chicken companions, to look to the sky and his inner abilities to soar, you also need to disregard the damaging and limiting influence of others. You need to look up to our Creator and seek His counsel in your individual life to become all you are meant to be. Soar, like an eagle, above the influence of this world, which tries so hard to take your identity away from you. Once you find your true identity and purpose in life, and once you taste flight, you will never return to the life of a spiritual chicken.

If you have lost your true identity, I want to tell you that it is not too late to recover it. God is waiting for you with His arms wide open. God is a gracious, loving God.

○•●•○

"Father, forgive me, for I have lost my true identity. Help me to not be a victim of Christian Identity Theft. Please restore me back to Your family. Amen."

Chapter 2

THE WORK OF THE MASTER

"For we are God's workmanship..."
(Ephesians 2:10)

A TRUE MASTERPIECE

AS I WAS FINISHING MY UNDERGRADUATE degree in college, I took an art class. I had some electives to take before I could graduate, so I chose this "easy-A" class. Of course, little did I know that "easy" art class would be one of my hardest classes that quarter. I did not expect I would have to spend so much time outside class time for my projects.

However, through this experience, I learned that brain function improves. I realized that if a human being sets their mind to something, by God's grace, they can do it and be successful at it. Paint. Write music. Learn a new language. Learn to cook. Anything! If you want to do something, and you work for it, you can accomplish it! Whatever it is. It might take a while, but it will work.

If you have one talent, you will have two; and if you have two talents and dedicate them and use them for the Lord, soon you will have four; and if you have five, soon you will have ten, and so forth. If you are faithful, you will get what you do not have. And we can then create our own masterpieces in life. Thanks to this class, I could make nice art pieces that I could be proud of.

I appreciate different types of art, and I love museums! I like to see the magnificent pieces of art. Surrealism is my favorite style, so one of my favorite artists is Salvador Dali. I just love how weird his paintings are. When I look at his paintings, I immerse myself into the art, and I lose myself. When one looks at an art masterwork, you can't help but wonder how in the world could a human being put paint on a white canvas and make such amazing art.

When you perceive a masterpiece in person, it goes beyond the senses, beyond what we can comprehend. How can a human being produce something so amazing? How can a musician compose a piece that you experience, not simply listen to? How can a painter create an image that talks to you, and not one that you just see? How can an artist design something in which every person sees something different?

You know, someone authored a doctoral dissertation on Van Gough and added mathematical assignments to the different color applications in the order in which he would use them, and the numbers always add up the same in each painting. That is crazy! Because I do not think that Van Gough had a calculator and said, "*Does this add up in this painting? Oh, no! I'm off by one digit. I'm going to have to add green here. Ah... there we go!*" No! I am sure he did not do it that way. That is the thing with masterpieces! Sometimes they are unfathomable. But what is and what makes a masterpiece, after all?

There was an action going on, and the auctioneer pulled out an old, ugly violin and dusted it off. He asked, "*Do I have a bid? One dollar. Do I have two? Two dollars to the gentleman in the front. Three dollars, anyone? Do I have anything else? Any other bids? Come on people, anyone else?*" People saw that this violin was obviously old and in very poor condition.

At that point, an older man stood up in the back and asked the auctioneer, "*Sir, can I play it?*"

The auctioneer, being a smart guy, knew that if someone played it, he would most likely add some value to the instrument, so he agreed. "*Yes sir. Please come up front.*"

The old man passed through the middle of the aisle and made his way to the front. He grabbed the violin and dusted off a little more. He started tuning the violin and rosined the bow with some old rosin that was in the case. And then he played a beautiful piece that no one had ever heard.

A stunning melody filled the room, and other than the music from the violin, silence overflowed the building. As the elderly man finished playing the piece of music, he calmly put it back inside the case and said, "*Wow. This is a very nice violin! Thank you. I have no money, though.*" He got offstage and went back to his seat.

At that point, the auctioneer grabbed the violin once more and asked, "*Do I hear a thousand dollars? Two thousand? Do I hear three? Five thousand!*"

It sold for twelve thousand dollars. So, what made the difference? It was the touch of the master's hand. A masterpiece, therefore, by definition is something that is touched and/or created by a master.

THE MASTER IN ACTION

Well, check this out. At the beginning, God said, "*Let there be light.*" And there was light! "*Let there be trees.*" And guess what... there were trees! And so forth. He just spoke, and it happened. He commanded it, and it transpired. And suddenly, there were trees, plants, separation of land and water, fish, birds, and other animals. However, on the sixth day, things were different. It was not just a bunch of talk anymore. Oh, no! On that day, the Lord got His hands dirty! He got down on His knees close to the ground, and started playing with dirt.

Did you ever get in trouble for playing with dirt while you were growing up? I did. I used to have a white polo shirt as a uniform during elementary school. But believe me when I say that every day, by the time I got back home, my shirt was always maroon. My mom would have to do laundry daily, and I would get in trouble all the time because I would play with dirt.

Well, the Creator took His time and delighted with this piece in His creation. The Lord wanted to create His own masterpiece. He wanted to finish His Creation with a cherry on top. He wanted it to be in His own image. So, He started forming it with His own hands.

And I want you to realize something, and that is the fact that He did not simply make a mannequin figurine. It was not just a body model or a flab of mud. No! He took His time making every vein and artery, every organ with its specific function, and every cell within the body. His precision and meticulous care made certain the Creator missed nothing. And what He created was spectacular! Then He breathed His essence into this creature. And the Heavenly choir started singing as God finished this masterpiece.

And then God told the man, "*You are in charge now.*" I am pretty sure that Adam got happy to hear those words. Most men like to hear those words, right? He probably got all excited and said, "*That's right; I am in charge, baby!*" and did a little dance.

And then God told him to name all the animals. And I can just imagine that new human being just there, coming out with names for each of the surrounding creatures. *"I will name you... Zebra! Giraffe. Platypus? Hiphopanonymus... no, wait... Hippopotamus!"*

But soon the man saw that every living creature had a pair, someone to go to the banquet with. And he realized he was lonely. And he said, *"Wait a minute? What is up with this? The lion has a lioness, the tiger has a tigress, and even the platypus has a... female platypus. So how come there is no one for me?"* And he got sad. So, God hooked him up!

The Bible says that God put in Adam a heavy sleep. So, he moved his head like a pigeon, refusing to go to sleep, yawning and stretching his arms. Then he eventually fell asleep. And after that, way before modern medicine, God performed the first medical operation. He started opening the chest area, and He did not have to worry about E. Coli or any infections. So, God started with His business.

Now, I do not know about you, but I can just imagine God there smiling, telling Adam as he was asleep, *"Oh, boy, you don't even know what's coming! If only you knew the surprise that I have for you! Hehe..."*

Because I am certain that God took joy in creating us, His masterpiece. And so, He took out a rib. And no; He did not put any barbecue sauce on it. He was not about to eat it; you savage. But pay attention to this detail. To you and me, it was just a rib... you know, Adam's rib; but let us realize that this was indeed a rib in the hands of the Master. And with that rib He made a woman. And what a woman!

Now, I want to take the time to make a parenthesis here. Let us realize God did not create woman from a bone in Adam's foot, so that a man would trample on a woman in her dignity, for God did not intend that. However, let us also realize that God did not make women out of one of

Adam's head bones. So, women must not lower man or look down on him. As you can see, God believes in equal opportunity.

So, God knew what He was doing. God made Eve out of Adam's rib so that she could stand at and by his side. Side by side. Each with their own calling. A journey of uniqueness and togetherness, all at once. And we must understand this, that it was a rib just under his arm, so that he could hold her close to his heart. Who ever said that God is not romantic?

And so that was God's masterpiece—humankind, in God's own image. And He saw what He had done, and He knew it was good! You see, in every other day of the week, when God spoke and things happened, God saw it was good. This time, it was different. He *knew* it was good. We must pay attention to this detail. It was perfect!

And once again, the heavenly choir sang, for the Master had completed His masterpiece. Now, finally, Adam had someone to go to the banquet with. And right there, the first marriage began. A wedding, also a Divine creation. Then He told them, way before sin entered this Earth, "*Be fruitful and multiply!*" We are talking about an eternity of bliss as God created it.

THE CHERRY ON TOP

I want you to consider this wonderful reality. When your parents united in an act of love, twenty-three chromosomes from your mother and twenty-three from your father, carrying some 15,000 genes from each parent, joined. These genes, like letters of a divine alphabet, spell out the unique things that make you who you are—the color of your eyes, hair, skin, facial features, body type, personality, unique qualities, intelligence, gender, etc.

Within six to twelve hours of fertilization, the one cell had split into two, then four, then eight. Then all eight cells of 'you' journeyed down the fallopian tubes and settled into your mother's womb, and implanted into the uterine wall, where you grew at a fast rate.

After three weeks, your heart started beating. By four weeks, your arms and legs had appeared, your internal organs were growing, and you were 10,000 times larger than at first. By six weeks, your brain developed, and its signals could be measured. At three months, you were a beautiful little astronaut-looking creature moving in your watery capsule with unique fingerprints, closed eyelids, and translucent skin. And so it went, until some 266 days after conception, you were born, an intricate baby containing millions upon millions of cells, each with a specific function.

Psalms 139:13-16 says, "*For You created my inmost being. You knit me together in my mother's womb. I praise You because I am fearfully and wonderfully made; your works are wonderful; I know that full well. My frame was not hidden from you when I was made in the secret place. When I was woven together in the depths of the earth, your eyes saw my unformed body. All the days ordained for me were written in your book before one of them came to be.*" And Genesis 1:27 says, "*So God created human beings in His own image, in the image of God He created them; male and female He created them.*"

Every time I get a sundae, I put a cherry on top, as a statement of completion, and it adds an extra touch of awesomeness. Sometimes I even add two to make it better. Well, listen to this—you are the cherry on top in God's creation! He added two cherries too—male and female, after His own image. You are His masterpiece, created in the same image as the Master Himself. And do not let anyone ever tell you otherwise. You are worth everything! That is why you cannot go on in life destroying your body or living life with the belief that you have no worth or purpose.

People go through life doing horrible things, believing, "*Who cares? We are all going to die anyway.*" No! That is not the right philosophy to live by. God did not send His only Son so that we might die, but that we might live, and live abundantly! The Bible says that He who has the Son has life. He who does not have the Son, does not have life. So, choose life. It is not about what you know, but about Who you know. *"For God loved the World so much that He gave His only begotten Son, that whosoever believed in Him shall not perish, but have everlasting life! (John 3:16)"*

The question is, do you want Jesus in your life? Do you aspire to be restored to His image? He said that He went to prepare a place for you; but do you desire to be there with Him? The only way that you will not be there is if you truly do not want to be there. Many people argue that this is not true religion, and that this is simply cheap grace. But let me tell you, this is not cheap grace, but precious. In fact, a higher price has never been paid! It is the best of its kind because Jesus paid that ransom for you. That is genuine grace!

However, you must also live up to that standard of a masterpiece since you are representing the Master. I find it so ironic that there are so many people out there willing to die for something, for anything. My question to you is, are you willing to live for God? So, let Him walk with you. Let Him talk to you. Let Him convince you that you are His. You are His masterpiece, created in His own image. You are His pride and joy. You are the cherry on top of Creation. So, commit and surrender all to Him right now.

○●●○

"Father, thank You for making me a masterpiece! I pray that I may live in such a way that everyone sees Jesus, my Creator, when they see me! Amen."

Chapter 3

YOUR REAL IDENTITY

"See what kind of love the Father has given to us, that we should be called children of God; and so, we are. The reason why the world does not know us is that it did not know Him."

(1 John 3:1-2)

SEVEN CONFUSED MEN

ONE OF MY FAVORITE BOOKS IN THE BIBLE IS *The Acts of the Apostles.* I think that if written today, it would be called the *"Dreams of the Apostles,"* or the *"Strategic Plans of the Apostles."* But it is the *"Acts of the Apostles"* because in the book of Acts, you see the people of God *doing* extraordinary things. And I want to suggest to you that their story is our story. In fact, someone once said that history is prologue. That which has happened before precedes that which shall happen again. I believe that what God has done in one situation, He can not only do it again, but even top it next time.

We serve a God that is not locked by precedents. Just because God did something amazing before, in the past, it does not mean that He cannot do it again. Even more, He can do it even better the next time. I believe in a God that goes beyond what we can imagine, beyond what we can think. We serve a God that is the same God of the apostles—these people, ordinary, like you and me, that did amazing acts to uplift the name of the Lord.

I want to make reference to one story from this book of Acts, in chapter 19 and beginning in verse 11. It says, *"God did extraordinary miracles through Paul, so that even handkerchiefs and aprons that had touched him were taken to the sick, and their illnesses were cured, and the evil spirits left them."* Wow! Paul was one cool dude. I mean, can you imagine that? It says here that God did extraordinary miracles through him, even his handkerchiefs had some sort of power.

Imagine Paul walking down the street, and suddenly, he drops his handkerchief. Then someone who was sick was walking behind him, minding his own business, and as soon as he stumbled upon the handkerchief, he was cured. Crazy! Paul was so full of the Holy Spirit that even random objects that touched him had the power of God.

Verse 13 continues, *"Some Jews who went around driving out evil spirits tried to invoke the name of the Lord Jesus over those who were demon-possessed. They would say, 'In the name of Jesus, whom Paul preaches, I command you to come out.' Seven sons of Sceva, a Jewish chief priest, were doing this. One day, the evil spirit answered them, 'Jesus, I know, and I know about Paul; but who are you?' Then the man who had the evil spirit jumped on them and overpowered them all. He gave them such a beating that they ran out of the house naked and bleeding."* They were asked, *"Who in the world are you?"*

In this chapter, as I talk about identity, I ask you the same question: "*Who are you?*" As you read this chapter, I want you to keep this question in mind. Who are you?

Now let us go back to the story. In this story, we find seven young men who had some identity issues. They were known as the "Seven Sons of Sceva." Now, I do not know if you were ever in a gang, but that sounds like a gang name to me. Can you imagine? "*We are the Seven Sons of Sceva! Fear us.*" But these were seven young men who were confused, even though they grew up in the Church. How do we know this? Because their dad was the Senior Pastor! And these guys got the idea that it would be nice if they could be like Paul and make a living by casting out demons. And that is why they would say, "*In the name of Jesus—whom Paul preaches—I command you to come out.*"

It is amazing how one can get away with foolishness for a certain amount of time. However, eventually, it always catches up. These guys had witnessed the power that Paul had available to him. After all, the Bible says that they were "*extraordinary miracles that God did through Paul.*" They had witnessed how handkerchiefs and aprons that were simply touched by Paul could heal the sick, and even the evil spirits left those affected by them.

The problem was that they did not understand what it took to get that kind of power. So, they saw Paul doing amazing things, but they did not comprehend that the power was not Paul's; the power was God's. And they did not know how to tap into the Power Source. You see, they, like so many people today, wanted power without paying the price.

Have you ever noticed these people who always want to get into those get-rich-quick schemes? And then they always want you to join them too. They invite you to see a "good" video, and then you show up expecting to see a movie, and instead it is one of those pyramid schemes for a product they are selling. And it says, "*If you just put in your $100, then it will make you rich too.*" And what I am always wondering is, "*Well, how come it has not made you rich yet?*" But that is how we are. We want to get there quickly and without effort.

We live in a fast-everything society. We want to drive through life and get rich. And in our spiritual life, too. We want to cruise through it, order it, and then it happens. But we need to understand that to be successful, it takes hard work and commitment. Like the saying goes, "*There is no gain without pain.*" There is no prestige without a price. There is no glory without guts. There is no success without sacrifice. You do not get something out of nothing. And that is what these seven sons of Sceva were trying to do.

To have that kind of power, however, you need to connect to the Power Source that is God. It is a personal affair. You need to do it yourself. You need to know Jesus personally. You cannot live your spiritual life through your parents, or through your teachers, or through your friends, or through your pastor. It does not work by association. You need to connect to God! He needs to be *your* God.

And there they were, "*In the name of God, whom Paul preaches...*" They did not know Him for themselves. They hoped that by mere association, they might be successful. They hoped that just by being around in the environment of power, it would rub off on them. They thought that by simply being there, at the right time and the right place, but for the wrong reasons, they would get collateral blessings and get Divine power. But their words had no meaning; they were going through the motions, simply faking it.

But do you know what? Every time you think you are fooling somebody, it always comes around to get you. And maybe they might have gotten away with it for some time, but one day, one of the evil spirits responded to them. This demon said (paraphrased from Acts 19:15):

"Now, wait a minute! Hold on, guys. I know what power is. I mean, I used to be in Glory. And Jesus, I know... because He was here, and He beat us a few times. In fact, I was one of those demons that had to get inside the pigs. So, I know Jesus. In fact, I was one of those demons whom He told to 'shut up.' I know Jesus! We thought we had Him, but on the third day He came up out of that grave triumphantly. So, I know Jesus! He is the One Who said, 'All power be given into Me... death, power, and life are mine.' I know Jesus! He made the blind man see, the cripple walk, and even resurrected the dead. And let me tell you, that is power! When there was a storm, He said, 'Peace, be still' and the storm died. I know Jesus! He fed five-thousand with a few fish and a couple of bread slices. I know Jesus! He is able to love and forgive those that are oppressed. So, Jesus, I know.—And do you know what? I know about Paul too. He preaches like a mad man. Every time he goes to a town he turns it around. I know Paul. Put him in prison, and he has the nerve to break out in praise. I mean, he is so full of the Holy Spirit, that stuff that just touches him heals people. So, Jesus I know. And Paul, I know. But... who are you? Who in the world are you?"

WHO YOU REALLY ARE TRULY MATTERS

Not knowing who you are is dangerous. You see, it only takes one day. Eventually, your façade will be discovered, and the truth will come up. And so, I ask you once again, *"Who are you?"* The Bible says that they could not answer that question. And funny enough, it also says that the man who had the evil spirit jumped on them and beat them up too! And this was not just a regular beat-down; it was so bad, that these guys left running naked. It is there in the Bible. That must have been a scene!

So, the devil will mess you up. He will tell you, "*Come on. Come on...*" And one day, *boom!* He will expose you. "*Who are you?*" How would you answer that question? That is what the world is asking you too. Who are you?

How would you answer? Would you say, "*I am a Christian.*" So what? What difference does that make? Or how would you answer that question? Perhaps you would say, "*I am a man.*" "*I am a woman.*" "*I am a student.*" "*I am a husband.*" "*I am a father.*" "*I am a leader.*" "*I am a hard worker.*" How would you answer that? Does it even make a difference? Do you even know who you truly are?

We have a tendency to believe that just by being in the environment, we are saved. We actually believe that simply because we go to church, we are Christians. But let me tell you, just because you go to church does not mean that you are a Christian—just like going to McDonalds does not make you a Big Mac. And here is the thing, we can be in the Church all our lives; but so, what? You might still not even know who you truly are. It is so interesting how people say, "*I have been in the Church all my life. In fact, I was born a Christian!*"

But that is not true. Let me tell you why. Because to be a part of it, you must be born again. So, it does not work that way. It is not determined by association, church attendance, or length of time. And you must know who you are because so many things in the world are trying to steal your real identity.

FOUR BIBLICAL LESSONS ON IDENTITY

Let me tell you how to protect your identity. I want to share with you four Biblical fundamentals that you need to know, because they will help you with this Identity Theft issue that Christians face. I am going to tell you, Biblically, who you truly are, and Whose you are.

32

1. You Are A Masterpiece

The first thing you need to know is that you are made in the image of God. We covered that in the previous chapter. This is what the Bible says in Genesis 1:26-27, "*God said, 'Let Us make man in Our image, in Our likeness, and let them rule over all the Earth.' So, God created humankind in His own image, man and female, He created them.*" You must know you are made in the image of God.

It might not feel like it sometimes, but you are a masterpiece. It is essential for you to realize and never forget that you are, indeed, made in the image of the Creator of the Universe. God could have said, "*Let there be man,*" like the other things created in that first week. But He took His time, kneeled, got His hands dirty, and formed us in His own image.

I understand that at some point in your life perhaps you were not treated as a masterpiece. Maybe growing up, you were one of those that people used to tell called 'ugly' or perhaps you simply did not fit in. But let me tell you this, whether this was your experience or not... just because some people might not recognize your value, it does not mean it is true.

You are a masterpiece! If I were to get a $100 bill and crumple it and throw it in the ground and step on it, and then ask you how much it is worth, you would know that it is still worth $100 dollars, right? Just because it has been mistreated does not mean it has lost its value. You understand the point. You are a masterpiece, no matter what you have been through. And when we see each other, we must see God in each other.

2. You Belong To Him

I will expand this second point in the following chapter. But this is the second fundamental truth about your identity. It is found in 1 Corinthians

6:19-20. It says, *"Do you not know that your body is the temple of God? You are not your own."* You do not belong to yourself. You do not own your own breath. You belong to God! He paid a price for us. And it is a fact that we belong to Him twice.

First, we belong to Him because He made us; and twice, because He died for us. So, we are twice His. Can you imagine buying back what you made? If I were a famous artist who made a masterpiece, and then some dealer wanted to sell it to me, I would say something like, *"No way! You are crazy! I am not paying anything for that. I made it. It belongs to me already."* But God still paid the price for us.

As harsh as this sounds, I want to let you know I do not believe in self-esteem. I am sure that many people have told you to instruct children and youth to have self-esteem; but that is garbage. And before any of you fellow psychologists, sociologists, anthropologists, and counselors out there condemn me, let me tell you why. It is not self-esteem that we need, because the Bible says that we must die to self. What we need to have is Christ-esteem! It is Christ, the hope of glory. It is Christ in me, Christ in you. When you have identity issues, you cannot turn to yourself.

You cannot turn to your "good" self-esteem. You cannot turn to your money. You cannot turn to your looks. You cannot turn to how well you play basketball or soccer. You cannot turn to yourself. You must turn to Christ! So, you must have a Christ-esteem. You must realize you do not belong to yourself or to your parents or to your partner; you belong to God. And you belong to Him twice!

You need to get up every morning knowing the fact that Jesus made you. And like Job said, you should also say, *"Thank You, Lord. For even though words can destroy this body, I know my Redeemer lives! And what You made in me once, You can do again, and make it better. I can be born again. So, thank You, Jesus!"*

3. You Are Chosen

The third thing you need to know is found in 1 Peter 2:9. It says, *"But you are a chosen people, a royal priesthood, a holy nation, a people belonging to God, that you may declare the praises of Him who called you out of darkness into His wonderful light."*

You are a chosen person. In fact, in the original language, it says and means *"God's special treasure."* You are God's special treasure, indeed, and you have royal status because He chose you. That is great news! So, before you can act, before you can witness, and before you can share, you must recognize who you are. God chooses you for a purpose.

There was a young girl by the name of Samantha, and she was in the fourth grade. She was adopted. She knew it and did not have a problem with it. But when her classmates found out that she was adopted, they started mocking her. Any time that something bad happened, they would blame it on her saying mean things like, *"I bet it was Samantha. It is all her fault because she is adopted."* Or any time one of her classmates got a poor grade in a quiz, they would say out loud, *"Well, at least I am not adopted like Samantha."*

They were all so mean to her. One day, she went crying home and told her parents what was happening in school. Her parents told her something that changed her life forever.

The next day when she got to school, when her classmates started taunting her, saying, *"Here comes the adopted one! Here comes the adopted child,"* she responded. *"So what? My mommy told me I was chosen. She went through a bunch of other babies on many lists, and she did not choose any of them; she chose me. So, I was chosen. But you... you were all just a coincidence! You all just happened. My parents chose me; yours just had you."* And she shut them up for good.

It is the same with you. God chooses you, Himself, for a purpose. You are not a mistake or simply a coincidence! No one is an "oops" baby. He picked you up out of a lineup and redeemed you. He gave you His last name and His royal status. Never let people take away that royal identity from you. You are a chosen one! You are somebody. You are God's princes and princesses.

4. You Are An Heir To God's Glory

And finally, the fourth thing you need to know to protect yourself from Christian Identity Theft is found in Romans 8:15-17. It says, *"For you did not receive a spirit that makes you a slave again to fear, but you received the Spirit of sonship. And by Him we cry, 'Abba Father.' The Spirit, Himself, testifies with our spirit that we are God's children. Now, if we are children, then we are heirs—heirs of God and co-heirs with Christ, if indeed we share in His sufferings in order that we may also share in His glory."*

No matter what is going on in your life, the Holy Spirit, Himself, testifies that you are, indeed, children of God, heir to His glory. You are a child of God, and you will receive the glory that was promised to those who trust in Him. Do you also want to claim that inheritance that God wants to give you as His child? That is your blessed hope. You can come to Him and call him "Daddy." And I will also expand on this point in an upcoming chapter.

I want to remind you that you are royalty. You are the king of all creations. And even though the enemy out there is trying to take away that identity from you, remember that you are God's. But to know who you are, to must first realize Whose you are. So, do not let your identity be stolen. Know who you really are: (1) you are a masterpiece, (2) you belong to Him, (3) you are chosen, and (3) you are a child of God, an heir to His glory.

The devil will tell you that you are something else, but he is a liar. Do not believe him. Claim your destiny as a child of God, live out your status, and represent God well in everything you do and everywhere you go. And then, and only then, will you be able to respond with confidence when the devil asks you, *"Who are you?"* You can say, *"I am a child of God. I belong to Him. So do not dare to mess with me."*

○●●○

"Father, please help me embrace and never forget my real identity. Amen."

Chapter 4

AN ISSUE OF OWNERSHIP

Know that the LORD is God. It is He who made us, and we are His;
we are His people, the sheep of His pasture."

(Psalms 100:3)

IDENTIFICATION

ANYWHERE YOU GO AROUND THE WORLD, you'll find that ID's are very important. They show who you are. They tell who you belong to. For example, mine says I belong to the County of Orange, to the state of California, to the Olivarría clan, etc. In fact, IDs are so essential in our lives, that people even get fake IDs. We have established already that identity theft is one of the biggest problems we face today.

And that is why we must always carry our identification cards everywhere we go. My question to you is this: What does your ID of life say about you? Does it say that you are a mechanic? A student? A skateboarder? A musician? A teacher? To whom or what does it say that you belong to?

OF CATS AND DOGS

Let me share something about myself. I hate cats! There. I said it! I really, really dislike them. Besides the fact that I am allergic to them, I believe that the only reason they exist is to show us that not everything in life has a purpose. When God created them, He was probably like: *"I was just kidding guys... but do not worry, there won't be any of those in Heaven!"* To me, cats are the living proof that God has a sense of humor. (Please don't hate me or stop reading this book.)

But here is the interesting part... the problem is that my wife loves them! She's always had at least one. To make matters worse, when we started dating, she had the fattest cat that I had ever seen in my life. This cat eventually passed away from old age. (Don't feel bad; we have two now!) But I remember when my wife and I were dating and how we would have arguments about cats and dogs.

I still remember the first time I saw this cat, too. It was bigger than a normal dog! In fact, she also had two dogs at the time, and they were afraid of this cat. It was so huge and fluffy! Have you seen the movies of "Shrek"? Well, imagine that cat, Puss In Boots, although gray and white, instead of orange and white, but the size of Shrek! I am not kidding. It was a giant-sumo cat. Her name was 'Xena,' like the warrior-princess.

But you see, as a kid, every time I saw one, I just wanted to strangle it because of the allergies I would get. And it appeared as though for a short period of time, it was infested with cats where I grew up. It was like a plague, an epidemic, or something of that sort. Therefore, I have always believed in that old saying that says, "He that lies down with cats will rise up with fleas." I even dislike the way they walk. They are just so conceited!

My wife once asked me why I dislike them so much, so I thought about it. This is what I told her, "They simply have no purpose. I mean, think about it... what can cats do? At least dogs can be used in different ways, like, for example: (1) for protection. But have you ever seen a "Caution: Beware of Cat" sign? Not unless it's in a zoo. Or imagine being chased by a cat! Also, (2) for guidance. Blind people use dogs to guide them. But what could a cat possibly do? I mean, have you ever seen a blind person guided by a cat, with a leash? That'd be a sight! Also (3) for "go-for's." Dogs bring back bones, sticks, balls, etc. I mean, sure, some dogs might bite your leg off, but at least they will bring it back! But try playing fetch with a cat! Good luck. And lastly, (4) for driving in the carpool. One could put a hat on a dog while driving so that you could go into the carpool lane! But try doing that with a cat! I mean, if cats could talk, I am sure that we would find it even harder to get along with them; they just are so into themselves!"

My wife was not very thrilled or convinced with my argument. So, you see the dilemma I was in. I love my wife, but I cannot like cats... even hers! Because if I did, it just would not be me!

It was crazy the day I met Xena many years ago. By this time, we had been dating for some time, but I had not had the "opportunity" to meet her fat cat. You see, I had told her I would not like her cat, so I warned her not to leave me alone with her, because I just would not know what could happen. But the day came. It was an interesting encounter. We got to her house, and even though I could not see it, I knew the cat was somewhere close, because I could sense it.

My anti-cat feelings (otherwise known as allergies) became strong. My wife, who was my girlfriend then, disappeared somewhere upstairs, as I remained by the entrance.

And there it came, so suddenly, out of the corner... walking straight towards me. It was as if she knew who I was. I guess my wife had had a talk with her previously. Xena came to me, walking all cocky, as cats usually do. And I got scared! I was frightened, because up to this point in my life, I had never seen a cat that big or fat. I mean, other than in the zoo, of course. In fact, I was wondering if that was not an over-weight, midget panther instead.

And it came to me—my wife had left us alone so that we could make peace, to talk face-to-face, man-to-cat. And I kid you not; she walked around my legs, rubbing herself to my legs. I literally thanked God that I was wearing jeans. I wanted to kick her head off, but I could not, of course. Because if I did anything bad to her, I would be in so much trouble, you do not understand. So, I just "kindly" moved her with my foot and pushed her away. I mean, I wasn't planning on picking her up, you know.

But I could not hate it. Well, at least, not as much as I would do with any other cat before! But I told her, *"Look, Xena, just for the sake of your owner I will not kill you or put you in the microwave! Just for the sake of your owner, I will not hate you! And listen, it is not because of you, you ugly cat, but only because of whom your owner is! So, you better feel special, punk, because you are not like any other cat. And it's all because of the love I have for your owner!"*

And then I kicked her away like a soccer ball towards the wall. No, just kidding. Things were cool between us from then on. As long as she stayed a few feet from me, and I from her, it was all good. And again, all because of whom she belonged to. It was not about her, but about her owner.

IT IS A MATTER OF OWNERSHIP

Now, I turn to you. To whom do *you* belong? Pay attention when I tell you this—we all belong to God! For us to be free, Jesus Christ paid a price so high that we could have never paid off. Paul reminds us, *"Do you not know that your body is a temple of the Holy Spirit, Who is in you, Whom you have received from God? You are not your own; you were bought at a price.*

Therefore, honor God..." (1 Corinthians 6:19-20). And then again in the following chapter, *"You were bought at a price..."* (1 Corinthians 7:23).

I believe that there is no greater hunger in the human heart than the hunger to belong—to belong to someone, to know that there is a safe place, to know you belong as you are, accepted as you are, to know that you will be given all you need, and to belong and know that no one can take you away from that place. That is why gangs are so successful in recruiting young people.

However, that hunger is only filled when you become convinced you belong to God. When a person becomes convinced that they belong to God Who loves them, the God Who will let nothing separate them from His love, it releases within their life the greatest restorative, healing power on Earth.

And we *all* belong to God! It does not matter if you are big or small, tall or short, light or dark, brown, black, white, or purple, Jesus' blood covers all of us. With that price, we all now belong to Him. Revelation 5:9 says, *"And they sang a new song: 'You are worthy to take the scroll and to open its seals, because You were slain, and with Your blood You purchased men for God from every tribe and language and people and nation."*

Did you catch that? Read it again. *"And with your blood You purchased men for God from every tribe and language and people and nation."* We *all* belong to Him! It does not matter where you come from, because it is simply not about who you are, but about Who He is.

THE WORK OF THE ANTAGONIST

Satan has proposed to make you miserable! His purpose is making you suffer, to give you pain, and to make you fall. The way I acted towards cats represents how Satan acts towards humanity. For no reason, he wants you to feel pain, to hurt you, to keep you away from God, and to destroy you.

However, when he approaches you and he sees that the blood of Jesus Christ has washed you, and when he realizes you belong to the King of kings and the LORD of lords, he backs away! He cannot hurt you knowing that you are protected by your Owner! He is afraid of our Owner!

Jesus, Himself, said that we would have this problem. In John 15:18-19, He said, "*If the world hates you, keep in mind that it hated Me first. If you belonged to the world, it would love you as its own; however, you do not belong to the world, because I have chosen you out of the world. That is why the world hates you.*" But the good news is that just a chapter afterwards (John 16:33) He added this, "*I have told you these things, so that in Me you may have peace. In this world you will have trouble, but take heart! I have overcome the world.*"

So, you see, it is not who you are, it is not where you come from, and it is not the color of your skin, your height, or weight. It is simply not because of you. It is because of your Owner! But you need to always carry with you that ID, so that there is no question to Whom you belong. And you need to act accordingly as well. Peter reminds us, "*Be holy because I am holy... For you know that it was not with perishable things such as silver or gold that you were redeemed from the empty way of life handed down to you from your forefathers, but with the precious blood of Christ, a Lamb without blemish or defect.*" (1 Peter 1:16, 18-19)

SOME CLARIFICATIONS

I must be sincere with you. The truth is, I cannot guarantee that my wife's cat would still be around after our first encounter if I had not known to whom she belonged. I cannot guarantee she would still have all her hair on its body. Perhaps after just a few minutes, she could have been just a smelly ball of fur floating in the toilet. Who knows? (Just kidding, the truth is that I wouldn't hurt a fly!) But because of the sake of the cat's owner, I could not touch her! I just love my wife so much, I know it would only hurt her. And that is the least of the things I would ever do to her.

Now, you might say, "Wait a minute! Satan *does not* love our Owner, so your analogy is flawed." And you are right. Satan does not love our Owner, but he knows Him. And, oh boy, is he in trouble if he messes with us. He tries the impossible to bring us down, but it is only when we choose to back away from the arms of the Almighty, which is our Owner, when Satan succeeds in drowning us.

It is only when we allow Satan to become our owner when we fail. And Jesus is a great Owner! So why even run away from home, when He takes care of us, when He feeds us with His Word, and when He paid the price with His own death for us?

THE SUPREME OWNER

Let me tell you about what kind of Owner that we have. In Jesus Christ I see a God Who is like the father who told his son he would send him to sleep in the attic, with only bread and water for his supper, if he were disobedient once more. The child disobeyed his father again and was sent to the attic. The father could not eat. He had the boy in his mind and heart. His wife tried to console him. "*I know what you are thinking. But you must not bring him down from the attic. It would only cause him to lose respect for you and disobey again. Don't break your promise.*"

The husband replied, "*You are right; I will not break my word. But he is so lonely up there!*" He kissed his wife good night, entered the attic, ate bread and water with the boy. And when the child went to sleep on the hard boards, his father's arm was his pillow that night. That is the kind of Father, the kind of Owner that we have. We have an Owner committed to loving us, dedicated to blessing us, and delighted to protecting us. He is an Owner that will never fail.

I want to share a story with you that represents this message. It is the story of Team Hoyt. Team Hoyt is an inspirational story of a father, Dick Hoyt, and his son, Rick, who participated together in numerous marathons and triathlons around the world. Because of a complication since birth, Rick cannot walk or talk. When Rick was eleven, they took him to Tufts University to get rigged with a computer device that would help him communicate.

This device allowed Rick to control the cursor by touching a switch with the side of his head, one of the few parts of his body that he can move. Rick could finally communicate. One of the first things Rick said was that he wanted to run. While in high school, Rick convinced his father to push him in his wheelchair in a five-mile race. That day changed Rick's life. After the race, Rick typed, "Daddy, when we were running, it felt like I was not disabled anymore!" And that sentence changed Dick's life. From then on, Dick wanted to make sure Rick got that feeling as often as possible.

And since that day, Team Hoyt's achievements are amazing. For over four decades, Dick pushed, pulled, and carried his disabled son, Rick, through over 1,000 marathons, races, and triathlons. Dick also pulled Rick in cross-country skiing, taken him mountain climbing on his back, and once even hauled him across the entire United States on a bike. Dick passed away in 2021 at the age of eighty-on, and Rick passed away in 2023 at the age of sixty-one. I am lucky I had the opportunity to see them once. On an interview, Rick typed the words, "No question about it, my dad is the Father of the Century."

Dick Hoyt is an amazing example of how engaged our Heavenly Father is in our lives. When we were broken, he was our wings. When we could not keep going, He went for us. When we had to die because of our sins,

He took our place. So why would we even consider leaving Him, when He has been so good to us?

In her life, Xena ran away several times. My wife would always look for her and patiently waited for her to embrace her and provide her unconditional love. Xena would always come back, or she would be found unhealthy, dirty, and hungry—just like the prodigal son. Every single time, my wife would take her back, cure her wounds, clean her, and love her. During those times I would always think, "What a stupid cat! Why would she leave when she is so spoiled here?" And then it hit me; that is exactly what we do with God, our Owner. It is not worth running away.

A SIMPLE MESSAGE

The message is simple. It is all an issue of ownership. It is not because of who you are; it is all about Whom He is. And if you allow God to be your Owner, then you will all be all right. Do not wonder off from Him. And when I say that it will all be all right, I do not mean that you will not have problems. You will have more attacks from the enemy. Regardless, it is always better to be in a storm with Jesus than anywhere else in the world without Him. It is even better to be in a fiery furnace with Jesus, than anywhere else in the world without Him. Ask the disciples or Hananiah, Mishael, and Azariah (Shadrach, Meshach, and Abednego), and they will tell you.

And by belonging to Him, then you will say like Paul, "*If we live, we live to the Lord; and if we die, we die to the Lord. So, whether we live or die, we belong to the Lord.*" (Romans 14:8) So to whom do you belong?

∘•●•∘

"Father, please forgive me if I have left Your arms. Thank You for being a wonderful Owner. Help me embrace my role in Your Heavenly family. Amen."

Chapter 5

WHO'S YOUR DADDY?

"Jesus said to him, 'Have I been so long with you, and yet you have not come to know Me, Philip? He who has seen Me has seen the Father; how can you say, 'Show us the Father'?"

(John 14:9)

A FUNNY EXPRESSION

I AM SURE THAT YOU HAVE HEARD THE EXPRESSION "Who's your daddy?" This phrase has been used countless times in the media. This saying has also been exploited in apparel. I grew up playing sports. I remember whenever someone scored on someone else, they would say, "That's right! Who's your daddy?"

But what does it mean? When is it usually used? The catchphrase, rather than implying who your blood father is, basically refers to who has control of you, who owns you, who you respect and obey, etc.

Growing up in Mexico, I noticed something interesting about last names. Have you ever noticed how many Hispanic last names end in "*ez*"? As a kid, I used to wonder what the deal with that was. You see, in old

Spanish, "ez" at the end of a name meant "the son/daughter of." Therefore, Gonzalo's son would be called Gonzalez, Domingo's son would be called Dominguez, and so forth. In fact, many other languages have a similar mechanism.

For Armenians, it is the names that ends in "ian." The Poles use "ski." For the Irish, it is the names that begin in "O'" the Scots use "Mc." And it's even easier to see in modern day English, with Johnson, Williamson, and Robertson, for example. The Scandinavians are quite similar. You can even see the importance of who your father was even throughout the Bible. As you can see, for many centuries, men have identified a person by who his/her father was.

Do you remember the movie "The Lion King"? Of course you do! Who doesn't? Well, this movie tells the story of a young lion that is the son of the king. The lion runs away when his father dies in an "accident," and the cub feels responsible for that death. He takes refuge with a pair of insectivores, and we see how the king of the beasts is reduced to a life of eating bugs.

After some time, he has a dream, in which his dead father appears to him (if any are concerned by this because of spiritism, remember that this is a movie about animals that talk) and says, "I am your father!" No, wait. Wrong movie! That is Star Wars. I confuse my movies sometimes. He says, "Remember who you are."

You see, he had forgotten who he truly was. He was not a bug eater. He was the son of the king. He was a prince. He was the monarch of all creatures! He had forgotten who his daddy was. God says the same thing to us: "Remember who you are. I am your Father." Are you listening?

THE POWER OF DNA

Some time ago, the CBS broadcast program '48 Hours' conducted an exploration of the children of certain famous people and how they were influenced by what they saw from their parents while they were growing up. Laila Ali, daughter of Muhammad Ali, grew up surrounded by boxing. Even after her parents divorced and she moved away with her mother, Laila Ali still felt a strong influence from her father and aspired to follow in his footsteps of becoming a boxing world champion.

She eventually fulfilled that dream. One of her most notable fights came when she fought the daughter of another great boxer, Joe Frazier. The battle between Laila Ali and Jackie Frazier concluded the same way as the fight their respective fathers had in the seventies in Zaire (now the Democratic Republic of Congo)—Ali beat Frazier.

I want to let you know, however, that it is not just a matter of influence. It is at the core of who you are. Who you are is not just in the blood that flows through your vein. Your genes determine who you are. They determine how you look. You received traits—as genes—from both your parents. You have genetic material from both, which is why you look like both your mom and your dad. And I want to suggest to you that when Adam was created, he had the genetic material of God. Genesis 1:26 says, *"And God said, 'Let us make man in our image, after our likeness...'"* Adam had divine DNA engrained in him.

One of my cousins had an interesting occurrence on one particular day. He was already married and had two children with his wife. Well, on this day, his doorbell rang and there was a teenage boy at the door. "I am your son," were the words the boy said as he identified himself. You see, when my cousin was in high school, he had an encounter with a neighbor, whose family moved soon after to the south. They never saw each other again, and they did not stay connected. At some point many years later, that girl, now a grown woman, told her teenage son that he had a father back in California. My cousin never knew about this.

As the boy grew up, he met his real dad. DNA testing confirmed that my cousin was, in fact, the father. And before my cousin passed away, they had an opportunity to finally live life as father and son.

But who usually needs to use this kind of DNA service? Obviously, those that are not sure of who their dad (or perhaps, mom) is. Although, there are many who do not need to use it, even in such circumstances, because the family resemblance is clear.

Well, how do you know if God is your true Father? Is there some sort of spiritual DNA test? Check this out. Jesus says those who are God's children love the Son, Jesus (John 8:42), and they also obey Him (verses 43-47). In fact, in this story recorded in John 8:31-47, Jesus confronts some Jews and tells them who truly are God's children and who are not. Essentially, Jesus says that if we are God's children, then we must live as children of the King. You cannot go on living life as a spiritual insectivore.

Many people are asked who their father is, even in the Bible. In 1 Samuel 17, we see the story of when David kills Goliath. Right after, King Saul asks David, "Who is your daddy?" Verse 58 says, "'Who is your father, young man?' Saul asked him. And David answered, 'I am the son of your servant Jesse of Bethlehem.'" Jesus was also asked Who His father was.

In John 6:25-59, we see the story of some Jews wondering Who Jesus was. Verse 42 records them asking, "Is this not Jesus, the Son of Joseph, whose father and mother we know? How can He now say, 'I came down from Heaven'?" Jesus had just stated that it was, indeed, His Heavenly Father Who had sent Him, and they were still wondering Who really His Daddy was.

EARTLHY VS. HEAVENLY FATHER

Now, I feel the need to explain something. I want to make an explicit statement here. I know some people struggle with the idea of God as a Father. Many times, it is because of their own relationship with their earthly fathers. I, personally, am very proud of my father. Though he recently passed away, he was a wonderful man, in every sense of the word. He was a great example of what it means to be a good husband, a spiritual leader, and a true father. My brothers and I always considered ourselves lucky men. To me, the idea of God as a Father makes perfect sense. It is a beautiful analogy.

However, as stated above, I am aware there are many people who do not have a decent experience with their fathers. I know that there are some earthly dads who leave their kids and want nothing to do with them. Some even refuse to pay child support. Others simply want nothing to do with their child's life. And when someone has a dad like that, their reply to the question of who their daddy is, usually is, "I do not have one."

Many other people do not even know who their father is. Others would have preferred not to know, since their father was an abusive figure in their lives. Perhaps you are amongst the ones that find it difficult to associate God as a paternal male figure.

I want to tell you it is ok. This is a biblical analogy, but still an analogy indeed. And God is beyond our human correlations and comparisons. For us human beings, it is perhaps not possible to imagine what or how significantly different beings are since we always carry substances such as leftovers of our own experience into our imaginations. It is the same when we try to understand What, Who, or how God is. Not much is concrete about God to our logic; however, we can still speculate about His reality. All the ideas and images of God that we have are human constructions, and most of our reasoning about Him is based on inconclusive evidence. (However, this does not mean that He is not real or that it is impossible for

Him to exist simply because we cannot see His dimension or His own nature of reality.)

So, you see, we as God's creatures cannot approach the study of God without first understanding who we are as created human beings. Therefore, Theology goes together with Anthropology, since in order to relate to God we place on Him human perceptions. Our understanding of God is only through the human context. Therefore, all our models of God are human simulations that we relate to (e.g., "God is Father," "God is the Shepherd," "God is my Rock," "God is love," etc.).

But listen, Theology is about God with us and not just simply about God. God builds the analogies of His own existence for us to understand at least a small bit about Him; this is true Revelation—coming from Him towards us, and *not* the other way around. God is wholly and Holy Other. He is outside of all reality as we know it. And that is why the names and attributes we have in this world for God are metaphors and not concrete ideas.

But whatever relationship you have with your earthly father is not the main point, because you can always still have a great relationship with your Heavenly Father. That is why when Jesus was teaching the disciples to pray, He started with the words, *"Our Father in Heaven."*

In fact, these are some of the most well-known words in the Bible. Most Christians can quote at least the beginning of the Lord's Prayer. And what a privilege it is to address God in this way! "Our Father." Isaiah 63:16 says, *"You, Oh Lord, are our Father, our Redeemer...."*

WHAT IS YOUR SPIRITUAL DNA?

You must realize you have been adopted into the Family of God. When people ask you, "Who's your Daddy?" you need to respond with confidence, "God is my Daddy!" God wants more than anything to be your Father. Read the following verses:

❖ *"Yet, oh Lord, You are our Father. We are the clay, and You are the potter; we are all the work of Your hand."* (Isaiah 64:8)

❖ *"When my father and my mother forsake me, then the Lord will take me up and receive me."* (Psalms 27:10)

❖ *"Blessed be the God and Father of our Lord Jesus Christ, the Father of mercies and God of all comfort, Who comforts us in all our tribulation."* (2 Corinthians 1:3-4).

❖ *"Your Father knows what you need before you ask Him... Therefore, do not worry, saying, 'What shall we eat?' or 'What shall we drink?' or 'What shall we wear?'... For your heavenly Father knows that you need all these things. But seek first the kingdom of God and His righteousness, and all these things shall be added to you."* (Matthew 6:8, 31-33)

❖ *"All those who are led by the Spirit of God are sons of God. For you did not receive a spirit that makes you a slave again to fear, but you received the Spirit of sonship, and by Him we cry, 'Abba Father.' The Spirit Himself testifies with our spirit that we are God's children. Now if we are children, then we are heirs—heirs of God and co-heirs with Christ, if indeed we share in his sufferings in order that we may also share in his glory."* (Romans 8:14-17)

So how is your relationship with God, your Daddy? I use the word Daddy because that is biblical. The word 'Abba' means 'Daddy' in Aramaic. So, you see, when you come into the family of God, you do not come as a servant. You come as a son or a daughter and have a relationship that is close enough to call God your "Daddy," like Jesus did.

Paul said it best in Galatians 4:4-7, *"And when the time had fully come, God sent His Son, born of a woman, born under law, to redeem those under law, that we might receive the full rights of sons. Because you are sons, God sent the Spirit of His Son into our hearts, the Spirit Who calls out, 'Abba Father.' So, you are no longer a slave, but a son (or daughter); and since you are a son (or daughter), God has made you also an heir."*

Daddies are significant to us. They give us a sense of identity. They are supposed to provide us with a sense of security. They are the ones who are to provide for us in every important matter. However, there is no earthly father that is flawless. As I already established, no earthly father entirely fulfills the job description that God has set forth. No earthly father is without fault. Even those who are good fathers fail. As much as a try to be the best father possible to my children, I am aware that I am flawed.

And this is even more reason we need the Heavenly Father in our lives! He is not an absentee Father. If anything, *we* are absentee children! Sadly, many times we tell God that we want nothing to do with Him, unless we are in trouble or when we need Him. If someone is sick, call Dad; you need a job, call Dad; you do not feel good, call Dad; car broke down, call Dad... but the rest of the time, forget Dad.

Look at the parable of the prodigal son in Luke 15. That was exactly the son's reaction! It wasn't until he felt he needed his dad that he went to him.

In Luke 15, in the parable of the prodigal son, Jesus shares an outstanding depiction of what your Heavenly Daddy is really like. It is the story of a son who wasted everything—his inheritance, his opportunities, and his father's trust—, and ended up working and living with pigs. Through this story, Jesus shows how, even though you might waste opportunities and no matter how far you have fallen, the arms of your Daddy are still open, reaching out in love towards you.

Then the story says in verse 22 that *"then the father put a ring on his hand..."* In those days, the family insignia to endorse documents was on the ring. It represented the full weight of the authority or power invested in that family name. Thus, in teaching us to pray "*Our* Father" (Matthew 6:9), Jesus offers authority to us as God's partners.

That name is given to you fully and freely, with all the rights and privileges granted to you as a member of His eternal family. And not only Jesus, but also the Father offers an authoritative right to be sons. John 1:12 says, "*Yet, to all who received Him, to those who believed in His name, He gave the right to become children of God.*"

WHAT SHOULD WE DO AS HIS CHILDREN?

When a child imitates his daddy, he/she tries to be like him in every way—in what he does, in what he says, and in what he thinks. Well, you are to do the same; you must act like Him, talk like Him, and think like Him. Ephesians 5:1 says, "*Therefore, be imitators of God as dear Children.*"

When I was a kid, I always liked to wear my dad's clothes and work boots. In fact, I have pictures where my brothers and I are wearing something that belonged to my dad. We aspired to be like him. We wanted to act like him. He was our hero. And that is what we are called to do with our Heavenly Daddy. 1 Peter 1:15-16 says, "*But as He Who called you is holy, you also be holy in all your conduct, because it is written, 'Be holy, for I am holy.'*"

You can put any characteristic of God in there and fill in the blanks. For example, "Because I am holy, you should be holy... Because I love, you should love... Because I am compassionate, you should be compassionate... Because I am forgiving, you should be forgiving... etcetera.

The Bible also says in Proverbs 23:7, "*For as a man thinks in his heart, so is he.*" I am sure that you have heard the saying, "You are what you eat." Well, I would like to suggest to you that you are what you think. Although obviously, if you think you are Superman and try to fly off a building, it will not work, and there will be consequences. That is not what I mean. David Koresh thought he was Jesus, and that did not work well.

What I mean, rather, is that if you believe with conviction that you are a prince/princess because of Who your Daddy is, then you will act like one. You will behave as such. If you think of yourself like your Daddy thinks of you, then you will become what you think you are. And because God thinks of you as a loved conqueror (Romans 8:37), who can do all things through Him (Philippians 4:13), you should think that too.

How is your resemblance to your earthly dad? Do people tell you, "You are the living image of your dad"? Perhaps some people have told you, "You are identical to your dad when he was your age!" Many people tell me that. Now think, how is your resemblance to your Heavenly Daddy? Is your imitation of your Father a good one?

Remember, if you have suffered in this world, do not worry, for we have a hope in the adoption of God's family. Check out what Romans 8:22-23 says, "*For we know that the whole creation groans and suffers the pains of childbirth together until now. And not only this, but also, we ourselves, having the first fruits of the Spirit, even we ourselves groan within ourselves, waiting eagerly for our adoption as sons, the redemption of our body.*"

Go out now, and if the world tempts you, may the Spirit enable you to reply like Jesus did to His earthly parents when He was twelve in the temple. Luke 2:49 records Him replying, "*Didn't you know that I must be about my Father's business?*" Go out and proclaim without shame or fear Who really is your Daddy.

More than anything, always remember that He is your Daddy. You are not just a child of God—you are His offspring. There is a difference. You are not just a baby (although you might act as though that is exactly what you are); you are a mature adult, whose name is in His inheritance will. Live accordingly.

"Thank You, Daddy, for being the perfect Dad and adopting me into Your family! Amen."

Chapter 6

WHAT'S IN A NAME?

"To the one who is victorious, I will give... a white stone with a new name written on it, known only to the one who receives it."

(Revelation 2:17)

BABY NAMES

ONE OF THE MANY IMPORTANT DECISIONS confronting new parents is, "What shall we call our baby?" Most new parents spend hours debating this question. We all realize that names matter. Shall the new baby be named after his father, her grandma, a favorite friend? Should the baby be given a name that is popular now? Or one that simply sounds good? Perhaps something made up and original?

My wife and went through this process twice already when our son and daughter were going to be born. Like most new parents, we went through the long and arduous process of name-finding before they were born. There were agreements and disagreements. There was plenty of research done. And in the end, we agreed with names we were all happy with—including our kids (or at least we hope).

Names are important because once you pick a name, the child will be stuck with it for a long, long time! Babies have no voice in the selection of their names. They must live with them—to live them down or live them up. Names are also important because many times you become what your name represents.

Every so often, you'll run across a person with multiple names, such as Charles Phillip Arthur George Windsor. That's sounds odd until you discover that's Prince Charles. If you say that is a heavy load, remember he's royalty, and he needs a long name.

THE NAMES OF JESUS

And so it was with Jesus. Even before his birth, He had many names. The prophet Isaiah, writing seven hundred years before Jesus was even born, prophesied that the Messiah would have several names: *"For to us a child is born, to us a son is given, and the government will be on his shoulders. And He will be called Wonderful Counselor, Mighty God, Everlasting Father, and Prince of Peace."* (Isaiah 9:6)

This verse reveals four names for Jesus. Each one unlocks an aspect of His character. They teach Who He is and how He can help us today. These four names speak to us about wisdom, power, security, and assurance.

First, Jesus is the ultimate counselor, and as the Wonderful Counselor, He gives wholesome direction to His people. Those who follow Him will not walk in darkness, but in the blazing light of day. Jesus is also Mighty God. If Jesus was only a regular human, then everything that we as Christians is in vain.

But that is not the case! And because He is the Mighty God, we rely on Him. He is also the Everlasting Father, meaning He is before, above, and beyond time. He is the possessor of eternity. And all that a good father is, Jesus is to His people. Because He is like a father (already established in the previous chapter), He cares for His people. And because He owns eternity, He can give us eternal life. And lastly, He is the Prince of Peace. God's ultimate plan for peace rests not in treaties, or lessons, or progress, or material prosperity. God's plan for Peace is the Maker of Peace, Jesus, the Messiah.

So, in this one verse, we see the four names of Jesus, and this is what they mean to us today: If you are confused, He is the Wonderful Counselor. If you are weak, He is the Mighty God. If you are scared, He is the Everlasting Father. And if you are disturbed, He is the Prince of Peace. However, besides the names, the most important part of our verse is the first three words: *"For to us."* The gift of Christ is a personal gift from God to us. And a gift requires a response.

If I put a gift under your Christmas tree, you may acknowledge it, you may admire it, and you may even thank me for it. But it isn't yours until you open it and take it on your own. Well, God has a Christmas gift for you, not wrapped in bright paper and fancy ribbon, but wrapped in clothes and lying in a manger. It is the gift of His Son. It is for you! The gift is still there. It must be received.

However, at the Incarnation, God took the form of human flesh. That is why one of His names is Immanuel—God with us. Not only is Jesus just God, but He is also God with and within us. He is not some distant deity somewhere out there. He is here, amongst us. And that is why it is significant to understand the meaning of names.

BIBLICAL NAMES AND MEANINGS

The names in the Bible are more than just labels—they're windows into the personalities and destinies of the people they represent. Jacob was called that for a reason. And so was Adam. So, the next time you come across a name in the Bible, take a moment to ponder its meaning and how it reflects the character of the individual. And remember, just like Adam, Abraham, Jacob, and Mary, you too have a name and a purpose that are uniquely yours. Embrace it, own it, and live it out loud.

In the Bible, we see many instances where God changes someone's name to signify a new identity and purpose. One of the most famous examples is when God changed Abram's name to Abraham, which means "father of many nations." Can you imagine being called "father of many nations" before you even have a single child? Talk about pressure! But God doesn't stop there.

He also changes Sarai's name to Sarah, meaning "princess." Now, I don't know about you, but if God wants to call me a princess (or a prince in my case), I am totally okay with that! It's like getting a royal upgrade without having to deal with all the drama of a royal family.

And let's not forget about Jacob, whose name was changed to Israel, which means "he struggles with God." Again, I don't know about you, but if my name meant I was constantly struggling with God, I might have a few choice words for Him! But Jacob embraced his new name and became the father of the twelve tribes of Israel. Talk about turning a negative into a positive!

But what can we learn from these name changes? It's all about embracing our new identity and purpose. Just like Abram became Abraham and Sarai became Sarah, we, too, can step into the alternative names and identities that God has for us. The next time you're feeling down or discouraged, just remember two things: first, remember Who He is—the Wonderful Counselor, Mighty God, Everlasting Father, Prince of Peace, and God with us—, and second, remember that He has a new name and purpose waiting for you. Who knows, maybe you'll be the next "princess" or "father of many nations" in God's eyes!

OUR NEW NAME IN CHRIST

As Christians, we are blessed with a new identity through Jesus that is truly life changing. So, put on your spiritual name tag and reflect on the new identity you receive through Jesus.

First, let's talk about the amazing name we receive when we accept Jesus into our lives. No longer are we just plain old Jane or John—we are now children of the Most High God! That's right, we have been adopted into God's family and given a new name that reflects our true identity as beloved sons and daughters of the King. So next time that someone asks you who you are, just tell them you are royalty—no big deal.

But wait, there's more! Not only do we get a fancy new name, but we also get a whole new wardrobe to match. That's right, when we put on Christ, we are clothed in righteousness and adorned with the armor of God. So, say goodbye to those old rags of self-doubt and insecurity, and say hello to the fabulous new outfit of confidence and strength. Who knew that being a Christian could be so fashionable, right?

Now, let's not forget about the perks that come with our new identity in Christ. We are no longer slaves to sin and shame, but free to live in the fullness of God's grace and love. So go ahead, walk with your head held high and your heart full of joy, knowing that you are a new creation in Christ. And don't be afraid to flaunt your new name and identity for all to see. After all, you're a divine masterpiece, created for a purpose.

Let's take a moment to reflect on the incredible transformation that takes place when we accept Jesus into our lives. We are no longer defined by our past mistakes or failures, but by our new name in Christ. So, embrace your identity as a child of God, put on your spiritual name tag with pride, and go forth with confidence and purpose, knowing that you are loved, valued, and cherished beyond measure. Keep in mind that to know who you really are, you must first know Whose you are. And, my friend, you are a divine masterpiece, created by the Master Himself, so live your purpose out loud.

SCRIPTURAL EXPLORATION—REVELATION 2:17

In Revelation 2:17, we uncover the hidden treasures of scripture that can help us reclaim our stolen identities and live out our purpose with boldness and confidence. In this verse, we are reminded that God has a special name for each of us—a name that only He knows. It is a name that reflects our identity as His beloved children, His divine masterpieces. So, if you've ever felt like you've lost sight of who you really are, take heart! God knows your true name, and He is ready to reveal it to you in His perfect timing.

And not only does God have a special name for us, but He also promises to give us a white stone with a new name written on it. Now, I don't know about you, but I'm picturing a fancy personalized nameplate I can proudly display on my desk. Who wouldn't want a shiny new name to go with their shiny new identity as a child of God?

This means that we can walk in confidence, knowing that our past mistakes or failures do not define us. We are not who the world says we are, but who God says we are: His beloved, His masterpiece, His chosen ones.

Let's remember that the world does not define our identities, but God, Who created us, does. So, let's embrace our new names, our true identities as children of God, and live out our purposes with boldness and confidence. And if you ever need a reminder of who you really are, just look at that shiny white stone with your new name on it. It's like a personalized gift from God Himself, reminding you of your true worth and identity. So go ahead, reclaim your stolen identity so that you can truly live your purpose out loud!

○•●•○

"Thank You, Jesus, for giving me a new name with a great meaning and writing it in the book of life! Amen."

Chapter 7

JESUS LOVES ME THIS I KNOW

"We love Him, because God first loved us."
(1 John 4:19)

JESUS LOVES ME

THE CHILDREN'S SONG, "JESUS LOVES ME" is perhaps one of the most popular Christian songs around the world. Children from many cultures have sung it, and its message has affected many. This simple children's song is often one of the first songs learned by new Christians, and it is easy to understand why. In its simplicity, "Jesus Loves Me" gets right to the point with the most important thing to say of all, which is that Jesus loves you and me. And how do we know this? Well, the Bible tells us so!

This song has been translated into more languages than any other Christian children's song. Many missionaries favor it's simple and easy-to-remember chorus to explain the gospel easily to new converts. I remember singing this song "Jesus Loves Me" as a kid in both Spanish and English. The message of the song is very simple, and yet it is extremely profound:

Jesus loves me! This I know,
For the Bible tells me so.
Little ones to Him belong.
They are weak, but He is strong.
Jesus loves me! This I know,
As He loved so long ago.
Taking children on His knee.
Saying: "Let them come to Me."
Yes, Jesus loves me!
Yes, Jesus loves me!
Yes, Jesus loves me!
The Bible tells me so.

HOW MUCH JESUS LOVES YOU

I love springtime right after winter, especially here where I live in Southern California. I can see clear blue skies, green hills, white mountains in the distance, and palm trees throughout. It is a portrait example of how beautiful our world is. There is no doubt in my mind that God is an artist. However, even the loveliest scene on this planet does not even compare to the place where Jesus is and was before He came. And yet, He left all of that to come here for you and for me.

You must grasp this reality, because understanding God's love is crucial to discovering our purpose in life. And He loves you so much that He is going to prepare a place for you so that you can be together forever with Him. Jesus loves you so much that He died so that you might live.

Jesus proved His love, both in Gethsemane and in Calvary. Jesus loved you enough to go to the garden and await His captors so that you, the captive, could be set free. Jesus loved you enough to hang on the cross so that He could be lifted from the Earth and draw all men unto Him. Jesus loved you so much that He rose from death on the third day so that you could also one day rise to eternal life with Him.

His love is the ultimate source of all things good. It's like the chocolate chips in the cookie of life—without it, everything just falls apart. When we grasp the depth of His love for us, we can see ourselves as the divine masterpieces that we are. It's like looking in the mirror and realizing, "Wow, I'm a work of art—created by the ultimate artist!"

The love of Jesus is stronger than any pain you may experience, stronger than any failure you may have committed, stronger than any problem you may have to face, and stronger than any fault that you may have. Jesus loves you despite the things that you may have done. There is nothing you can do to make Jesus love you any less. His love is unconditional! It comes with no strings attached. He does not have to, but He loves you because He wants to.

In Ephesians 3:17-19 Paul uses the four dimensions to describe the love of Christ: width, length, height, and depth. These were the same dimensions given by ancient philosophers to describe the vastness of the universe. Paul uses this concept for us to understand the complete nature of the love Christ has for us. Literally, the love of Christ is so massive that it fills the entire universe. Then, in Romans 8:38-39, Paul reminds us that Jesus' love for us is so prevailing that there is absolutely nothing in the entire universe that can separate us from that love.

In John 15:9, Jesus tells His disciples about One Who personified the meaning of love. He says: "*As the Father has loved Me, so have I loved you.*" This verse is quite profound when we think of the love Jesus displayed while He was in this world. Think of the many times that multitudes insulted Him, all while having the power to destroy them with a single command from His lips. Or contemplate the masses of people who came to Him bearing sick loved ones and left His presence rejoicing. Consider the care and attention He paid to the unimportant, the oppressed, and the hated.

He showed His love to Peter, even knowing that soon he would renounce Him publicly. He even lived day after day and shared meals with the one who would betray Him! And despite all this, as prophesied, then came this universe's ultimate demonstration of love. Jesus died so that we might be saved! No wonder it says just a few verses afterwards in John 15:13, *"Greater love has no one than This that He lay down His life for His friends."*

Lastly, the verse of John 3:16 is a Bible verse that even non-Christians recognize thanks to those homemade signs at sports games. But let's dig a little deeper into this beloved verse and uncover the true power of God's love for us. John 3:16 serves as a reminder that no matter what we've done or how far we've strayed, God's love is always there, ready to welcome us back with open arms.

It's like having a divine safety net that catches us every time we fall (and let's face it, we fall a lot). Embrace John 3:16 as the ultimate love letter from God to us, His beloved children. Let it be a constant reminder of our true identity as cherished and valued members of His kingdom.

JESUS' DEMONSTRATION OF LOVE

We all know that Jesus was the ultimate example of love, but let's dive deeper into some ways He showed His love to others. Foremost, Jesus showed His love through His actions. Whether it was healing the sick, feeding the hungry, or simply spending time with those who were marginalized in society, Jesus went above and beyond to show His love for all people. He didn't just talk the talk; He walked the walk—literally.

One of the most memorable examples of Jesus' love is when He washed His disciples' feet. Now, let's be honest, feet are not the most glamorous body part to wash. Especially during that time! But Jesus got down on His knees and served His disciples in this way, showing them that love means putting others' needs before our own—even if it involves stinky feet.

Another way Jesus proved His love was through His forgiveness. Time and time again, Jesus forgave those who wronged Him, showing us that love means letting go of grudges and extending grace to others. I don't know about you, but I struggle to forgive someone who cuts me off in traffic, let alone someone who crucifies me.

So, as we reflect on Jesus' demonstration of love, let's remember that love isn't just a feeling—it's an action. It's about serving others, forgiving those who hurt us, and showing kindness to everyone we meet. And who knows, maybe if we follow Jesus' example, we can spread a little more love in this world—one stinky foot at a time.

A FAMILY'S LOVE

For the longest time, I could not understand such unconditional love. It would not make sense, until I learned from my family's example. My family has helped me at least comprehend the beginning of what it means to truly love unconditionally. And I am sure that most of you relate to this as well—perhaps in your own families.

I come from a first-generation immigrant family. There were originally five of us: two parents and three boys; I am the youngest (and I would like to think the coolest one) of the boys. We share a love shown by sacrifice. Let me explain. Growing up, we were encouraged to share with one another. Back in Mexico, we were never rich, though we lived well. Both my parents were professionals, so thankfully, growing up, we had everything we needed.

However, that changed with time. Things back home got tougher. Mexico went through a challenging economic breakdown in the mid-nineties, which caused my father to almost lose his construction company. Suddenly, we could not afford many things—including our education, since even though we lived in Mexicali (on the Mexican side of the border) we studied in Calexico (on the American side of the border). This meant that we earned pesos, but spent in dollars. This simply made it worse.

Chances were good that those nice shirts that my older brothers had, the ones I always liked, would one day come to me. As the youngest boy, I benefited the most from the "*hand-me-down enterprise*" mom and dad were running at home. For most of my growing years, I never knew what new clothes were.

Years later, when my oldest brother graduated from college, which was a huge financial sacrifice in it of itself, and started making some bucks, he remembered his two younger brothers. By this time, my other brother and I were in college, too. So, he would take us out to eat and have fun. I even remember once how we did not have money in our apartment to pay the bills, so we called him and he hooked us up, even though he had his own place somewhere else and had to pay his own bills in a different city working as a young teacher.

And then, of course, there have always been my parents. Talk about sacrifice. Mom and dad made tremendous sacrifices so that my brothers and I could attend private, Christian schools for most of our lives. You know how expensive that can be, especially with three kids! It was tough earning Mexican pesos, and then having to convert them to dollars to pay. The exchange ratio was ten for one at the time.

When we eventually moved to the US, they would each work somewhere around sixty hours a week, on average, to help us out and keep us in school. They worked so hard to supply all our needs. I remember how for several years my dad needed a pair of comfortable shoes, but he would not buy them until our tuition was paid. He would just use our old ones whenever we could get newer ones, even if they fitted him big, and they were all basically destroyed.

And there are so many other stories like that. Such demonstrations of sacrifice from my family while growing up have taught me much about what it means to love unconditionally.

Then, with time, I got married and started my own family. The idea of loving unconditionally took on new meaning after two life events: (1) marrying the love of my life and best friend, and (2) having my own children. When my son and my daughter were born, it released within me a never-experienced sensation.

When I first held my son and my daughter in my hands, seeing their fragile, yet beautiful bodies completely dependent on me, Jesus' love made even more sense. These newborns were a part of me. I was part of them. And I loved them, there and then, unconditionally and eternally. And I knew that there was nothing in this world that would ever keep me from loving them. I understood that there was nothing I would not do for them.

JESUS' LOVE CONVEYS IDENTITY & PUROPSE

The plan of salvation might sound complex, but it is not complicated. The words "Jesus loves me" are still the greatest theological truth of all times. Unfortunately, there are thousands of people who have left Christianity in what was called 'rebellion.' However, I would like to propose to you that many left because they were hungry for unconditional love. I wonder if many of them were ever shown, not just told, that Jesus loves them. I am curious if they were shown that God's grace is sufficient for them and that His love is one that never dies off, no matter what they have done. I wonder if they were told, "The world might hate you... but Jesus loves you!"

Many left simply because they were never taught or shown, or because they never fully understood that message of Jesus' unconditional love for them. But this is a message that we all need to know, because this message gives us hope. It is understanding this meaning that gives us an identity. It is knowing this that gives us purpose.

Many people find their identity and purpose in their image, their career, their ethnicity, their personality, their social status, their sexual orientation, political view, and/or their religion. They define themselves in a list of individual characteristics. But doing this ignores eternal consequences. Having only a shallow, earthly sense of identity relates to the lack of possessing an infinite purpose.

So, you must be certain that there is significantly more to life than this image that we create for ourselves. You must see beyond this limited existence and perceive your eternal identity. You must link your identity with God through His love. Enjoying a relationship with God gives you an important purpose with eternal consequences, and it also defines your identity as a child of God.

God does not want to see you miss out on your true identity as one of His children because He knows that this will only give you a misguided purpose in life. Do not live as an orphan, searching for belonging and purpose. You must realize because of His great love, God sent Jesus, His Son, to show us how to live a life that characterized a Godly identity with an eternal purpose.

Swiss theologian Karl Barth is one of the most influential Christian theologians in the past couple of centuries. Some consider his contribution to the Church and his influence to be unmeasurable. In 1962, Barth visited the United States to do a series of lectures at the University of Chicago and at Princeton Theological Seminary in New Jersey. At both locations during his talks, he was asked to summarize the theological implication of the six million words that he wrote in his four-volume opus, Church Dogmatics. Without missing a beat, on both occasions Barth replied, "Jesus loves me; this I know, for the Bible tells me so."

PERSONALIZING HIS LOVE

Have you ever stopped to really thinking about how much God loves you? I mean, He literally sent His Son to die for you. Talk about a grand gesture of love! It's the ultimate sacrifice. So, why not take a moment to internalize and personalize that love for yourself?

God's love isn't just some generic, one-size-fits-many love. No, it's tailor-made just for you. It's like a custom suit or a designer handbag—perfectly crafted to fit your unique personality and style. So personalize that love, make it your own, and wear it like a badge of honor.

And the next time you're feeling unsure of yourself or questioning your worth, just remember that the Creator of the universe loves you beyond measure. You are a Divine Masterpiece, a one-of-a-kind work of art, and God's love for you knows no bounds. Internalize and personalize that love, because you, my friend, are truly worthy of it.

Understanding God's love is like getting a GPS for your soul. It guides you towards your true purpose and helps you navigate the twists and turns of life with grace and confidence. So, the next time you feel lost, just remember that God's love is the ultimate compass pointing you in the right direction.

When we embrace God's love, we see ourselves and others in a whole new light. Suddenly, the annoying coworker becomes a beloved child of God, and that pesky neighbor becomes a fellow traveler on the journey of life. It's like putting on a pair of rose-colored glasses and seeing the world through the lens of love. And let me tell you, everything looks a lot brighter and more beautiful that way!

Understanding God's love is the key to unlocking our true purpose and reclaiming our stolen identity as divine masterpieces. So, let's bask in the warmth of God's love, embrace our uniqueness, and live our purpose out loud. Because when we do, we not only bring joy to our own hearts but also shine a light for others to follow.

A SIMPLE MESSAGE

No one will ever love you more than Jesus loves you right here and right now. Jesus has a love that can never be taken away from you. The message is so simple that we often miss it. Maybe it is because the idea that Jesus would love us unconditionally is sometimes beyond our ability to fully understand. I want to assure you today that the message of that song is true—Jesus loves you. Do you realize it? Do you understand what it means to know that Jesus loves you?

I am sorry to tell you this, but your partner's love will fail you, your boyfriend, girlfriend, spouse, and even children will fail you more than once. I am not prophesying; I am simply letting you know how it is, that is all. In fact, sometimes, even your parents' love will fail you too—as hard as that sounds. And as much as it hurts me to accept it, I am also aware I will fail my own children as a father.

However, Jesus' love for you and I will *never* fail. Never! So always remember this: *Jesus loves me! This I know, for the Bible tells me so.* In His love, you will find your true identity and a meaningful, eternal purpose.

○•●•○

"Thank You, Jesus, for Your unconditional love that provides me with an eternal identity and a meaningful purpose! Amen."

PART TWO

Purpose

Chapter 8

LOVING LIKE JESUS LOVES

"A new command I give you: Love one another. As I have loved you,
so you must love one another. By this everyone will know that you
are my disciples, if you love one another."

(John 13:34-35)

CREATED ON PUROSE AND FOR A PURPOSE

WHAT IS YOUR PURPOSE IN LIFE? Have you ever even thought about that? During the past years, emphasis on the word "purpose" became more common. We find titles such as Purpose-Driven this and that. But what is purpose, after all? Perhaps we need to establish that before anything else. According to the dictionary, "purpose" means: *"The object toward which one strives or for which something exists; an aim or a goal. Determination. Resolution."* But what do you think? What is purpose for you? Perhaps even more important, what is *your* purpose in life?

I have read that around fifty percent of Christians believe that happiness and personal fulfillment are their purpose in life. They believe

God put them on this Earth simply so that they could be happy and satisfied. But that is not what the Bible teaches. If we truly read, the Bible teaches us again and again that our purpose is to bring glory and honor to God.

The prophet Isaiah said: *"Everyone who is called by My name, whom I have created for My glory; I have formed him, yes, I have made him"* (Isaiah 43:7). We were made to bring glory to God; therefore, we are to glorify Him in all that we do with our lives. As the apostle Paul reminds us: *"We who first trusted in Christ should be to the praise of His glory"* (Ephesians 1:12). Paul also tells us: *"Whatever you do, do all to the glory of God"* (1 Corinthians 10:31), and: *"You were bought at a price; therefore, glorify God in your body and in your spirit, which are God's"* (1 Corinthians 6:20).

So, you see, our purpose is to glorify God. We should give some thought to that and ask ourselves: "How can I glorify God? Am I seeking God's will for my life? Am I seeking to walk the way He wants me to walk? Am I doing what He wants me to do?"

If we fulfill the primary purpose for which God created us, as a result, we will find what most of us are looking for in life: happiness, fulfillment, and reason of existence. We find these things not by seeking them, but by seeking the God Who made us, like Matthew 6:33 reminds us. As we come into harmony with God's purpose for us, everything else automatically falls into place.

That is why so many people who are seeking happiness or fulfillment, who are trying to find themselves, still live such empty, hopeless lives. They have not discovered the reason that God put them on this Earth, which is to know Him, to walk with Him, and to bring Him glory and honor. When we realize God created us and we try to fulfill that purpose, then we experience a joy and fulfillment in the Lord we have never known before.

So, I ask you once again, are you fulfilling the purpose for which God created you? In another verse, the apostle Paul summed up what his life was about and what should be the slogan for every Christian: *"For to me, to live is Christ, and to die is gain"* (Philippians 1:21). That is my purpose in life. Is it yours?

In this next section, we will delve into the idea of purpose. Now that we have discovered what our identity is, we can determine what our function is. I encourage you to fulfill that purpose that God created you for, and then truly you will be happy in life and everything that you do will bring you satisfaction. Remember that what we *do* is the best sign of what we *believe*. So let us live our purpose out loud.

JESUS EXAMPLE

As always, as we begin this journey of discovery of purpose, we should inspect Jesus' example. Jesus is the best example of selflessness and sacrificial love. I do not know who was the first one to declare that Christianity is about relationships and not behavior, but I know it was Jesus Who first practiced that idea.

Now, you might think: Jesus, the Son of God, is the ultimate example of love. How could we possibly measure up to that? Well, fear not, for we are not expected to be perfect like Jesus. But as we continue to delve into living a life of purpose, we can certainly strive to follow His example of loving others selflessly and sacrificially.

As we read in the last chapter, Jesus showed us time and time again that true love is not selfish or self-serving. He healed the sick, fed the hungry, and spent time with those who were rejected by society. And He didn't do these things for fame or recognition, but out of genuine love and compassion for others. So, the next time you hesitate to help someone in need, just remember what your purpose is and ask yourself—What would

Jesus do? Whether it's lending a listening ear to a friend in need or volunteering your time to serve those less fortunate, there are countless ways we can show love to others in our daily lives. Let's strive to follow Jesus' example and love others selflessly and sacrificially, knowing that our efforts are never in vain.

One of the most powerful examples of Jesus' sacrificial love is His ultimate sacrifice on the cross. He willingly gave up His life to save us from our sins, showing us that true love knows no bounds. While we may not be called to make the same sacrifice, we can certainly learn from Jesus' example and be willing to sacrifice for the well-being of others. Jesus' example of selfless and sacrificial love is a powerful reminder of the sort of love we are called to show others as Christians. So, let's take a page out of Jesus' book and strive to love others in the same way He loved us. Remember, we are all divine masterpieces, created with a purpose of loving and serving others.

But how do *you* love? Perhaps the question should be: Do you even love? I mean, truly "love." Think about it... *"All we need is love,"* wrote the songwriter from the Beatles... and in a way, he was right. But if there is a shortage of love in this world, it is certainly not God's fault. The New Testament tells us that the very reason for our being here is love. God is love. So, he or she who doesn't love then cannot know God.

A young woman and her grandmother were sitting on their porch, discussing a member of the family. "He's just no good," the young woman said. "He's completely untrustworthy, not to mention lazy."

"Yes, he's bad," the grandmother said as she rocked back and forth in her rocker, "but Jesus loves him no matter what."

"Well... I'm not so sure of that," the younger woman persisted.

"Oh, yes," assured the elderly lady. "Jesus loves him, I'm sure." She rocked and thought for a moment, and then added, "Of course, Jesus doesn't know him like we do, though."

Matthew shares with us the following story:

"*Now. when the Pharisees heard that he had silenced the Sadducees, they assembled together. And one of them, an expert in religious law, asked Him a question to test Him: 'Teacher, which commandment in the law is the greatest?' Jesus said to him, 'Love the Lord your God with all your heart, with all your soul, and with all of your mind. This is the first and greatest commandment. The second is like it: Love your neighbor as yourself. All the law and the prophets hang on these two commandments'*" (Matthew 22:34-40).

You see, we were created from love, for love, and to love. In fact, love is the very foundation of Creation. But love is not only at the heart of Creation; also, love is the reason for the Cross. We should not be surprised, then, that when Jesus was asked what the greatest commandment was, He answered without hesitation: "*Love the Lord your God with all your heart, and with all your soul, and with all of your mind. This is the first and greatest commandment. And the second is like it. Love your neighbor as yourself.*"

So, we can't escape the obligation to love, because when we stop loving, we cease to be humans. The problem is that most people love shallowly. That is that they only love those who love them. However, Jesus tells us to love differently.

LOVING LIKE JESUS IS DIFFICULT

Love is a powerful weapon. In fact, fear, greed, or love motivates most people. What are you motivated by? Is it love, or something else? Because let's be honest, loving like Jesus loves is not always easy. In fact, many times, loving is quite a difficult task. I mean, some people are very challenging to love, right? And others are just plain annoying.

But if Jesus can love us even when we mess up (and trust me, we mess up a lot), then we can show a little love to our fellow brothers and sisters in Christ. Remember that Judas went out to do his thing with "clean feet" because Jesus loved him and washed his feet. And if Jesus could love Judas, we can muster some love for that annoying coworker, that nosy neighbor, or that person is just "different."

Here is a true story. It is about a soldier who was finally coming home after having fought in Vietnam. He called his parents from San Francisco and said, "Mom and Dad, I'm coming home; but I have a favor to ask. I have a friend I'd like to bring home with me."

"Sure," they replied, "we would love to meet him."

"There's something you should know, though," the son continued. "He was hurt badly in the war. He stepped on a land mind and lost an arm and a leg. He has nowhere else to go, and I want him to come live with us."

"Oh, I'm sorry to hear that, son. Maybe we can help him find somewhere to live, though."

"No, I want him to live with us."

"Son," said the father, "you don't know what you're asking. Someone with such a handicap would be a terrible burden on us. We have our own lives to live, and we can't let something like this interfere with our lives. I think you should just come home and forget about this guy. We're sure he'll find a way on his own."

At that point, the son hung up the phone. The parents heard nothing more from him.

A few days later, however, they received a call from the San Francisco Police Department. Their son had died from suicide, they were told. The sad parents flew to San Francisco and were taken to the city morgue to identify the body of their son. They recognized him, but to their horror, they also discovered something they didn't know—their son had only one arm and one leg.

The parents in this story are like many of us here. We find it easy to love those who are good-looking or fun to have around, those who are not a "burden" to us; but we don't like people who inconvenience us or make us feel uncomfortable. We would rather stay away from people who aren't as healthy, beautiful, or smart as we are.

Thankfully, God won't treat us that way. He loves us with an unconditional love that welcomes us into His family, regardless of how messed up we are. And we must pray so that God will give us the strength we need to accept people as they are, and to help us all be more understanding of those who differ from us too.

In Jesus, God showed us the true way to love. Suddenly, God's love was given form, flesh, and substance. And there we find Him holding little children in His arms. There He is dining with Zaccheus, bringing love into a hated man's home. His arms are open in forgiveness without judging. His lips speak words of hope to those in despair. And finally, He hangs on a cross because of love. That is the way Jesus loves; and that is exactly how He wants us to love as well. He tells us: *"Love the Lord your God with all your heart, with all your soul, and with all your mind... and love your neighbor as yourself"* (Matthew 22:37, 39).

Sadly, our culture and our world today tell us to love ourselves and that's it... and maybe those who love us in return, though that's pushing it. But nothing more. Oh no, wait! It also teaches us to love our stuff, our material goods. But *not* other people—especially not those who differ from us. And that is exactly why we have so many broken families, a high crime rate, abused people, and children being raised by electronic devices. And the cycle starts all over again.

But 1 Corinthians 13:1 tells us that *"without love I am [nothing but] a noisy gong or a clanging cymbal."* Without love, we are just annoying and miserable, and life is pointless. Jesus tells us:

"I have come to bring you life, and life to the fullest... and I sure want to share it with you, but I can't give you that abundant life unless you love like I do. I want you to love Me above all things and above everyone, with everything that you are. And then I want you to love everyone else, even those you consider your 'enemies,' and I want you to do unto them like you would like to be done to you. Simply put, love them as yourselves! And when they are hungry, feed them, when they are in prison or sick, visit them, when they are in need, help them, pray for them, love them, and know that you are doing these same things unto Me as well."

That is what Jesus wants for us. He already showed us how to love like He does. Now He expects us to go out there and love everyone without exception. Don't label people. Don't reduce anyone. Because if God placed us in a category, all of us would fall under "un-savable." And we wouldn't want that, believe me. So, if a person is doing something wrong with his or her life, do not condone sinful living, but offer them a way out by recommending Jesus, with love rather than judgment.

Don't just preach against sin, but also offer them the One Who can save them from sin. Tell them about Jesus' unconditional love and encourage them to strive to live holy and strive to live right because they have a special Friend Who loves them no matter what. Let them know their sins are forgiven, and that they don't owe anything because Jesus paid it all.

John 21:15-17 presents an interesting conversation between Jesus and Peter. It says:

"When they had finished eating, Jesus said to Simon Peter, 'Simon son of John, do you truly love Me more than these?' 'Yes, Lord', he said, 'you know that I love You.' Jesus said, 'Feed My lambs.' Again, Jesus said, 'Simon son of John, do you truly love Me?' He answered, 'Yes, Lord, you know that I love You.' Jesus said, 'Take care of My sheep.' The third time He said to him, 'Simon son of John, do you love Me?' Peter was hurt because Jesus asked him the third time, 'Do you love Me?' He said, 'Lord, you know all things; You know that I love You.' Jesus said, 'Feed My sheep.'"

Jesus asked one of His closest disciples three times in a row if he loved Him, and if he loved Him more than anybody else. And Peter even got upset! *"Well, duh, of course I love You, Jesus! I'm here with You, am I not? I mean, I'm like one of your closest disciples. So, what's up with these questions?"* To which Jesus simply responded: *"Well, take care of my people then."* And today it is not me, but Jesus, Who is asking you: *"Do you love Me? Do you truly, honestly, love Me more than anyone and anything else, including yourself? And if so, how do you love Me? Do you show your love towards Me by loving my people?"* And then He tells you: *"If you truly love Me, love my people as well and take care of them. All of them!"*

PRACTICAL APPLICATIONS

In John 13:34-35, Jesus tells His disciples to love one another as He has loved them. Jesus set the bar high with His love. I mean, He died for us. And let's not forget about the second part of that command in verse 35—Jesus says that our love for one another will be a testimony to the world that we are His disciples. So basically, if we're not loving each other, we're failing our discipleship test. No pressure, right?

But hey, look on the bright side—at least we have a clear roadmap for how to live out our faith with purpose. Love God and love one another. It's simple, yet so profound. You cannot love by accident or by mistake; you must love intentionally. And since we now know that loving is not an option, but a commandment, let's now talk about how you can put this into practice.

First things first, let's talk about patience. I know, I know, it's not the most exciting topic, but trust me, it's essential to love others like Jesus. Remember that time Jesus waited three days to raise Lazarus from the dead? Yes, that's the patience we're talking about here. So, next time your coworker is driving you crazy, just take a deep breath and channel your inner Jesus.

Next up, forgiveness. We all know Jesus was all about forgiveness, even when He was being nailed to a cross. So, the next time someone cuts you off in traffic or steals your parking spot, try to remember that forgiveness is key to loving others like Jesus. And hey, maybe even throw in a little prayer for that person while you're at it. Who knows, you might just change their life.

Forgiving means letting go and not insisting on getting even. It means understanding that God will do the judging and leaving that to Him. Paul said, "*Beloved, do not avenge yourselves, but give place to wrath; for it is written, 'Vengeance is Mine, I will repay,' says the Lord*" (Romans 12:19). He also adds, "*Don't let the sun go down on your anger*" (Ephesians 4:26).

So, forgiving also entails not using your daily energy or time to dwell on who offended you. Do not do yourself or others disservice! While it is true that you cannot control what other people say about you or do to you, you can still choose how to respond. Do not give them the power to own you by not forgiving and by holding grudges. Do as Jesus would do. I know it's easier said than done, but we can try this daily.

Another practical way to love others like Jesus is by serving them. Jesus was all about serving others, whether it was washing His disciples' feet or feeding the hungry. So, next time you see someone in need, don't just walk on by—lend a helping hand. Whether it's volunteering at a soup kitchen or simply holding the door open for someone, serving others is a surefire way to show them the love of Jesus. We are all called to serve others. You can either do it with a good attitude or a bad one. It is your choice.

And finally, don't forget to show kindness and compassion to everyone you meet. Jesus was the epitome of kindness and compassion, so why not follow in His footsteps? Whether it's smiling at a stranger on the street or listening to a friend in need, acts of kindness can go a long way in showing others the love of Jesus. With a little patience, forgiveness, service, and kindness, you can show the world the true meaning of love.

But I want to talk more about this last point because compassion and kindness are difficult to give away because they keep coming back. In fact, the best way to beat boredom is to do generous acts to others without expecting repayment or compensation. Have you noticed why Jesus was never bored? Tired maybe, but never bored.

A few years back, I went to a work lunch meeting. The meeting didn't go as I'd like, and it put me in a gloomy mood. While driving back to the office, I decided to listen to the radio. As I turned it on, a jam was playing—Barry White's "Can't Get Enough Of Your Love Babe." Now, you must understand I love this song, plus I hadn't heard it in a while.

So, excitedly, I cranked up the volume and started singing along with Barry loudly. I figured this would change my mood. Music has always had the power to change my mood. And thankfully, it did. So, there I was, singing in my best baritone voice, trying to match the low of Barry's tone.

Now, something of importance to note here is the fact that the AC in that old car (which I got rid of years ago) wasn't working, so I drove with my windows down, since I live in warm Southern California. It was early September, and the air was arid, so all my windows were down to help with the lack of AC.

I pulled up to a red light, and without thinking too much about it, I continued with my high-volume, low-voice vocal performance. Quickly, I turned to my left and noticed a man next to me in a fixed-up muscle car, who also had his windows down. He turned and looked at me. He was an older Latino man, with salt-and-peppered slick hair and tattoos on his face. He sported a nice goatee and large, dark shades that covered part of his face.

Suddenly, I became self-conscious of the situation. I rarely care much about what people think and/or say about me; but this time it really hit me! Afraid that I'd stared too long, I turned back my gaze towards the road in front, and in a swift movement, I lowered the volume of my radio.

Thankfully, this guy was a cool sport. I immediately heard as he turned his volume up, and little did I know, he was also listening to the same station! As the light turned green, I turned to him. He smiled and nodded. Of course, I'd stopped singing when I lowered the volume, though the song continued. But before we took off, he began to sing the song enthusiastically from that point on as he drove off. It was as if I had "tagged" him, and now he was it.

This encounter made my day. I returned to work with a full stomach and a smile in my heart. And no bad news from work would take my spirits down that day. From that day forward, every day, I strive to turn to someone I encounter and "tag" them. I try to make their heart smile and have them pass it on.

So, I encourage you to do the same. Let's make this world a better place by reaching those around us and doing something great for them today. They can then pass it on. Do random acts of kindness each day without expecting anything in return. You can start with your loved ones, but try to expand towards strangers eventually, anyone you come in contact with. Don't miss opportunities to love! Don't wait; start today. Make this a great day for someone else. It'll bring you joy as well.

This is the love reaction that John 13 talks about. *"As the Father has loved Me, I have loved you. The same way, now you love one another."* And this should be your mission, because love, not time, heals all wounds. People are made to be loved and things are made to be used. But that is why there's so much chaos in the world: people are being used and things are being loved. In fact, I know of several people who have left the church because they didn't feel loved—even if they knew it had the Truth.

If appropriate, hug someone at least once a day. Hugs do not need equipment, special batteries, or parts; just open your arms and open up your hearts. Be vulnerable and love away. Learning to love means being able to be vulnerable, as it comes with a willingness to confront risk. But vulnerability is not a weakness; it is strength! So, be strong in Jesus' love.

1 Peter 4:8-11 commands us to *"above all, love each other deeply, because love covers over a multitude of sins. Offer hospitality to one another without grumbling. Each of you should use whatever gift you have received to serve others, as faithful stewards of God's grace in its various forms. If anyone speaks, they should do so as one who speaks the very words of God. If anyone serves, they should do so with the strength God provides, so that in all things God may be praised through Jesus Christ. To Him be the glory and the power for ever and ever. Amen."*

BEING LOVING AND LOVABLE

I want to finish this chapter with this story. At a fund-raising dinner for a school that serves learning-disabled children, including this kid named Shay, Shay's father shared this story. Shay and his father would take walks in the afternoon because the doctors had said that it would be good for him to be taken outside for a walk and to breathe fresh air. Several times, during some of these walks, Shay and his dad had walked past a park where some boys he kind of knew from the neighborhood were playing baseball.

On one of those occasions Shay asked, "Do you think they will let me play?" Shay's father knew that most boys would not want him on their team. But the father understood that if his son were let into play, it would give him a much-needed sense of belonging.

Shay's father approached one boy on the field and asked if Shay could play. The boy looked around for guidance from his teammates. Getting none, he took matters into his own hands and said, "We are losing by six runs, and the game is in the eighth inning. I guess he can be on our team, and I'll try to put him up to bat in the ninth inning."

In the bottom of the eighth inning, Shay's team scored a few runs but was still behind by three. At the top of the ninth inning, Shay put on a glove and played in the outfield. Although no hits came his way, he was ecstatic just to be on the field, grinning from ear to ear as his father waved to him from the stands.

At the bottom of the ninth inning, Shay's team scored again. Now, with two outs and bases loaded, the potential winning run was on base. Shay was to be the next at-bat. Would the team let Shay bat at this stage and give away their chance to win the game?

Surprisingly, Shay was given the bat. Everyone knew a hit was all but impossible because Shay didn't even know how to hold the bat properly, much less connect with the ball. It was obvious he didn't know what in the world he was doing. However, as Shay stepped up to the plate, the pitcher moved a few steps to lob the ball in softly so Shay could at least be able to make contact. The first pitch came, and Shay swung clumsily and missed.

The pitcher again took a few steps forward to toss the ball softly toward Shay. As the pitch came in, Shay swung at the ball and hit a slow ground ball to the pitcher. The pitcher picked up the soft grounder and could have thrown the ball to the first baseman. Shay would have been out and that would have ended the game. Instead, the pitcher took the ball and threw it in a high arc to right field, far beyond the reach of the first baseman.

Everyone started yelling, "Shay, run to first! Run to first!" Never in his life had Shay ever made it to first base. He scampered down the baseline, wide-eyed and startled. Everyone yelled, "Run to second Shay! Run to second!" By the time Shay was rounding first base, the right fielder had the ball. He could have thrown the ball to the second baseman for a tag. But the right fielder understood what the pitcher's intentions had been, so he threw the ball high and far over the third baseman's head. Shay ran towards second base as the runners ahead of him deliriously circled the bases towards home.

As Shay reached second base, the opposing shortstop ran to him, turned him toward third base, and shouted, pointing with his finger in the right direction: "Run to third! Over there!" As he rounded third, the boys from both teams were screaming, "Shay! Run home! Run home, Shay!" Shay ran home, in slow motion—but as fast as he could, then he stepped on home plate, and was cheered as the hero for hitting a "Grand Slam" and winning the game for his team!

"That day," said the father softly with tears now rolling down his face, "the boys from both teams helped bring a piece of the Divine Plan into this world by showing unconditional love to my son."

That is the sort of love that the world really needs. We need people who will take time to love like Jesus did. So, I tell this to you: "Love those closest to you but do more than that—walk in the footsteps of Jesus! Learn to love every person with whom you come into contact. As crazy as it sounds, but that kind of love can still save this world."

In his book, "The Amazing Laws of Influence," King Duncan says, "*One life touches another life and potentially both lives are changed; that one touched life touches another life and potentially the entire world is changed.*" And it all starts with loving God first, and then your neighbor like yourself. And that is the power of love; it multiplies exponentially!

1 John 4:20-21 says, "*If anyone says, 'I love God', yet hates his brother, he is a liar. For anyone who does not love his brother, whom he has seen, cannot love God, whom he has not seen. And he has given us this command: Whoever loves God must also love his brother.*"

God loves you not because you are flawless or not because you are a perfect person, because you are far from it! He loves you just because you are. And as a response to His amazing love, He wants you to love others the same way. So, love like Jesus did. And by doing so, do not let your identity be stolen.

Claim your destiny as a child of God, live out your status, and represent Jesus well in everything you do and everywhere you go by loving the way He has called us to do so. Love the way He wants you to love, so that others can see Him in you and so that there is no doubt you are one of His disciples. May your purpose in life be to make this world a better place, one person at a time.

Be a loving and lovable individual. One of my all-time favorites quotes in Christian writing is that of Ellen G. White in *Help in Daily Living*, pg. 2. She says, "*the strongest argument in favor of the Gospel is a loving and lovable Christian.*" Now, I don't know about you, but that is exactly what I want to be said of me after I am gone, that I was loving and lovable, just like Jesus. When we love others unconditionally, we reflect the love of Christ to the world. And guess what? People notice.

Your actions speak louder than words, and when you love like Jesus, you shine the light of God's love for all to see. So, keep loving, even when it's hard, because the world needs more love, now more than ever. And while it is true that you cannot reach everybody, you can reach somebody. The greatest impact that the Christian Church can have in this world is a loving and lovable Christian. Be that great impact in the world, for that is your God-given purpose.

○•●•○

"Dear Jesus, teach me and help me to love like You do. Amen."

Chapter 9

A PIECE OF THE PUZZLE

"Just as a body, though one, has many parts, but all of its many parts form one body, so it is with Christ."

(1 Corinthians 12:12)

UNIQUE ROLES WITH A BIGGER PICTURE

IN 1 CORINTHIANS 12:12-27, the apostle Paul reminds us we are all unique and essential parts of the Body of Christ. You are not just a random toe or a forgotten elbow. You are a vital organ, a crucial piece of the puzzle that is God's grand design. Now, some of you might be thinking. "But I'm not that important! I'm just a little pinky toe in the grand scheme of things." Let me stop you right there. In verse 22, Paul says, *"On the contrary, those parts of the body that seem to be weaker are indispensable."* That's right—even the pinky toe has a crucial role to play.

In verse 25, Paul tells us that there should be no division in the body, and that its parts should have equal concern for each other. So, next time you feel like the big toe is getting all the attention, remember that we are all in this together. We are a team, a family, a united front against the forces of darkness. We must support each other, lift each other up, and celebrate each other's victories—even if that means cheering for the pinky toe occasionally. Sometimes it's easy to look at others and wonder why you don't have it all together like some of them do. But your purpose is not to imitate others. Embrace your uniqueness and stop playing the comparison game.

In verse 27, Paul declares, "*Now you are the body of Christ, and each one of you is a part of it.*" And let me remind you, you are not just a random assortment of body parts; you are a masterpiece, a work of art crafted by the Master Artist Himself. You are fearfully and wonderfully made. You are not a mistake or an afterthought. You are a vital part of God's grand design.

Have you ever tried to complete a puzzle, only to find out that it's not complete? It's a horrible feeling. You will search everywhere for the missing piece because completing the puzzle requires all the pieces. When we discard or lose a piece, the complete picture suffers. 1 Corinthians 12:12 says, "*The body is a unit, though it is made of many parts; and though all its parts are many, they form one body.*" And in the Body of Christ, we need everybody—every part—every piece! With every individual piece, we are stronger. Even if just one piece is missing, we are lacking.

Consider the fact that God's plan is like a giant puzzle, with each person playing a unique piece. You may feel you're just a tiny corner piece, but without you, the puzzle would be incomplete. You were God's idea. A good idea, indeed. After creating us, the Bible mentions He said, "*It is good!*" Now, that's something!

It is for this reason that you must embrace your role, no matter how insignificant it may seem, because God has placed you in that position for a reason. And in a puzzle, no piece is unimportant. So, know that you are an essential part of God's grand design. Embrace your unique role and live it out loud, because the world needs your special touch.

Just like in a puzzle, each piece is unique in its shape, size, and color, in the same way, with the Body of Christ, our individual differences are not a weakness, but a strength. Each of us combined makes a beautiful picture. But if all the pieces were the same, it would be a boring picture. 1 Corinthians 12:17 says, *"If the whole body were an were an eye, where would the sense of hearing be? If the whole body were an ear, where would the sense of smell be?"* Every part is necessary for the whole.

Sometimes we feel different, and can't see how we fit, but that's okay. God has made you and placed you into this world with a purpose. God said to Jeremiah, *"Before I formed you in the womb I knew you, before you were born, I set you apart; I appointed you as a prophet to the nations"* (Jeremiah 1:5). He says the same to you today. And 1 Corinthians 12:18 adds, *"But in fact God has arranged the parts in the body, every one of them, just as he wanted them to be."*

Each person has a unique, tailor-made role in God's plan. Yes, that's right—you are not just a cog in the machine of life, but an individual with a specific purpose to fulfill. While you might have doppelgangers out there in the world, God doesn't make duplicates. You are one-of-a-kind! Just like a snowflake or a fingerprint, there is no one else on this planet quite like you. So, embrace your uniqueness and realize that you have something special to offer to the world that no one else can.

However, in a puzzle, one piece is not more or less valuable than the other. In the same way, in God's Kingdom, every part plays a specific role and fills a divine purpose. 1 Corinthians 12:15-16 explains that our worth is not determined by which piece we are. We can't say, "If I'm not an edge piece, then I'm not part of the puzzle." We also can't say we don't need a certain piece! (1Corinthians 12:21) We need to value those around us and each of us needs to do our part. Other people's purposes are tied to ours. Ephesians 4:16 says, *"From Him the whole body, joined and held together by every supporting ligament, grows and builds itself up in love, as each part does its work."* So, understand that even though your purpose is unique, it is connected to that of your neighbors.

Even though we live in an individualistic culture, we must understand nobody exists in a vacuum. Humans connect to God and to each other. And speaking about this, remember that united we attract, but divided, we distract. Think about this. Imagine that I throw a one-thousand-piece puzzle on the floor in front of you. What statement do those one thousand pieces make? What picture does it make? But now imagine that I show you the puzzle box top, with the complete image. Which image makes more sense? In our mission, we become more effective when we find another person to hook up with. Then another, and another, until we paint the entire picture of the gospel.

The corporate identity of the church has ramifications for everyone, and each one must understand their place in the Body of Christ. Paul uses the "body" metaphor in 1 Corinthians 12 to show us how much we need one another and the importance of every member. In fact, most of the metaphors about the Christian Church have a group identity involved: kingdom, bride, body, royal priesthood, sheepfold, building, etc. An individual citizen, priest, sheep, stone, etc., cannot perceive his or her identity without a correct understanding of the group. Our importance and value come in relationship to God and others, not in individual consciousness.

In John 17, Jesus prays for unity, not uniformity. Unity is not about agreeing, but about how we disagree. When we have a common core and a common goal, our differences are irrelevant. Jesus prayed for just one thing. He prayed for believers' unity, so that through this unity of

Christians, there would be such an impact in the world that they would believe that God the Father had indeed sent Jesus. What could Jesus have prayed for in the last moments before His arrest? I can think of a few things. For example, He might have prayed for His own strength, or that His disciples wouldn't abandon him and support Him, or perhaps that they would not flee from Him and His teachings after this crucial moment.

However, instead, His prayer was dominated by a single great thought: the unity of the disciples. You see, Jesus knew the Church could never make the impact on the world that He wished it to make, unless spiritually the world saw in that Church a 'oneness'—a unity.

Only the obvious visible unity of believers will convince the world of the divinity of Jesus. Only the sight of united disciples will convince the world of the truth of Jesus' message and mission. That is why John 13:35 says, "*By this all men will know that you are My disciples, if you love one another.*" So, unity not only benefits us inside, but it is also the best testimony for those outside the Church. However, it is important to know that unity is not uniformity. It does not mean that we must all be the same! In our diversity, we must unite.

One reason Christianity frustrates the world because they only see a fragmented, broken, disgruntled picture. Just a piece. But our unity paints a picture that attracts others to Christ! When they see and hear us worship together, we give them a glimpse of heaven. Not any of us can individually convey all the attributes, beauty, love, and compassion of Jesus. It takes all of us to do it.

We are effective when we stay connected because what we can't do alone, we can accomplish together. So, remember that God has a purpose and plan for you that no one else can fulfill and that your piece is essential in the greater picture, but don't forget that you are but a piece of it all.

SPIRITUAL GIFTS

In 1 Corinthians 12, before speaking about the different parts of the Body of Christ, Paul speaks about spiritual gifts. Verse 1 says, "*Now, about the gifts of the Spirit, brothers and sisters, I do not want you to be uninformed (ignorant).*" Let's jump to verses 4-11 add, "*There are different kinds of gifts, but it is the same Spirit that distributes them. There are different kinds of service, but it is the same Lord. There are different kinds of working, but in all of them and in everyone it is the same God at work. Now, to each one the manifestation of the Spirit is given for the common good. To one there is given through the Spirit a message of wisdom, to another a message of knowledge by means of the same Spirit, to another faith by the same Spirit, to another gifts of healing by that one Spirit, to another miraculous powers, to another prophecy, to another distinguishing between spirits, to another speaking in different kinds of tongues, and to still another the interpretation of tongues. All these are the work of One and the same Spirit, and He distributes them to each one, just as He determines.*"

Okay, so far right here, Paul is saying that in the Body of Christ, we all have unique gifts. And he says that these are gifts, talents, and skills that the Holy Spirit has given to each of us as He believes its best in the Kingdom. And all are needed.

Spiritual gifts are like superpowers. They're the tools that equip us for our roles in God's Kingdom. It's like being handed a big, shiny sword and being told, "Go forth and slay some spiritual dragons!" Okay, maybe not quite like that, but you get the idea. Imagine if every Christian had their own unique spiritual gift. It would be like a real-life version of The Justice League or The Avengers, but with less spandex and more prayer. Some people might have the gift of teaching, others the gift of preaching, and so forth. It's like a spiritual potluck—everyone brings something different to the table.

Here's the thing, though... sometimes we don't realize we have these gifts. It's like being given a Ferrari and then trying to drive it like a lawnmower. We need to explore and discover our spiritual gifts so we can use them to their full potential. Otherwise, we're just sitting on a goldmine of supernatural spiritual ability and not even realizing it. But when we embrace our spiritual gifts, we're like a well-oiled machine. We're firing on all cylinders and operating at peak performance.

It's like upgrading from an old flip phone to the latest smartphone—suddenly, everything runs smoother and more efficiently. Spiritual gifts equip us for our roles and help us fulfill our purpose in God's Kingdom. So don't be afraid to explore and embrace your spiritual gifts. So, dust off those spiritual gifts and put them to good use. You never know what miracles you might pull off with a little divine aid.

In Romans 12:4-8, Paul adds, *"For just as each of us has one body with many members, and these members do not all have the same function, so in Christ we, though many, form one body, and each member belongs to all the others. We have different gifts, according to the grace given to each of us. If your gift is prophesying, then prophesy in accordance with your faith; if it is serving, then serve; if it is teaching, then teach; if it is to encourage, then give encouragement; if it is giving, then give generously; if it is to lead, do it diligently; if it is to show mercy, do it cheerfully."*

Paul says here once again that we are all different. We have diverse talents, backgrounds, and experiences. And that is beautiful! We must appreciate this diversity within the body of Christ. This diversity reflects God's creative design. God intentionally created us differently and unique. That is because different talents fulfill different specific needs and purposes. You see, diversity enriches the community. And because of this diversity, we can have different perspectives, ideas, and ministries. We can approach problem-solving in a much better way. But in the end, diversity means nothing if we are not united.

And it also means nothing unless you do your part. See, Paul here is also saying that whatever your part is, you must do it to the best of your ability. If your gift within the church is giving, give generously. If it is serving, serve to the best of your ability. If it is teaching, then do that with joy. Whatever your gift is, do it greatly. Be yourself. Share your individual gift. Your unique gift cannot reach everyone. Be aware of that fact and be ok with it. Accept it. Deal with it. Do not take it personal. Your unique gift will, however, reach several and will impact them. And in relation to lessons on individuality, I have three quotes from famous historical people for you:

- ❖ "Whenever you find yourself on the side of the majority, it is time to pause and reflect."—Mark Twain
- ❖ "Be yourself; everyone else is already taken."—Oscar Wilde
- ❖ "Your time is limited, so don't waste it living someone else's life."—Steve Jobs

THE KEY INGREDIENT

In 1 Corinthians 12:31, Paul makes a significant shift in his conversation about body parts and spiritual gifts. After a long discussion regarding these, he says, *"Now eagerly desire the greater gifts. And yet I will show you the most excellent way."* And that is how chapter 12 ends and chapter 13 begins.

Why is this important? Let me explain. You see, back then, there were no divisions of chapters or verses. When Paul wrote this letter to the Corinthians, he didn't put "Chapter 12" then "Chapter 13" as titles. No! It was all one long letter. And right here is how he transitions into what we now know as the "Chapter of Love."

So, 1 Corinthians chapter 13 only makes sense when you understand what Paul has been talking about right before. He is talking about the Body of Christ! He is talking about unity. He is talking about how to use your God-given talents. And now, he finally goes into what is the key ingredient, the glue that unites all of this. The key element that brings the body together—which is love. Do you see how it all comes together now?

My question to you is, what is your talent? What is your Spirit-given spiritual gift with which you can contribute to the Kingdom of God? And what part of the body are you? Have you ever thought about that? I invite you to consider that. Because you are important. We've established that already. And the body needs you, and it needs you to do your function well, to the best of your ability. There is a beauty and strength in diversity, and the world needs your unique gift. Yes, you! So, bring your talent and serve God. But do it all with love. Because, otherwise, Paul says in chapter 13, it's just noise. It's no longer harmony or beautiful music, but just an annoying noise, if you don't do it with love.

Each of you and I are different. We are all unique. And that is great news! God has given us special gifts for the service of others and for the greater benefit of the world at large. I don't know what part of the body I am. Probably the pinky on the left foot. But even I have my function in this body. And I am important too. However, if I don't do my part, then the whole body suffers. Have you ever hit your small toe as you walk by something? It's horrible! I mean, the whole body suffers, right? So, I echo Paul, and invite you to do *your* part in this world.

Strive to make the world a better, happier place, one person at a time. Fulfill your mission with your unique, God-given gifts. Whether you are a toe or an armpit, do your part faithfully. Connect with others and paint the picture of Jesus to the world. And most importantly, do it all with love. That is your purpose!

"Dear Jesus, help me do everything with love, including using my gifts, playing my unique part in Your Kingdom, and showing Your picture to others. Amen."

Chapter 10

LIVING UP TO THE STANDARD

"Do nothing out of selfish ambition or vain conceit. Rather, in humility value others above yourselves, not looking to your own interests but each of you to the interests of the others. In your relationships with one another, have the same mindset as Christ Jesus: Who, being in very nature God, did not consider equality with God something to be used to His own advantage; rather, He made Himself nothing by taking the very nature of a servant, being made in human likeness. And being found in appearance as a man, He humbled Himself by becoming obedient to death—even death on a cross!"

(Philippians 2:3-8)

PRODUCING GOOD FRUIT

A CHRISTIAN IS SOMEONE WHO FOLLOWS Jesus Christ as their Lord and Savior, and strives to live their life under His teachings. In fact, the word "Christian" literally means "follower of Christ." My question to you is, do you reach the measurement? Striving to imitate Jesus and living according to a high standard. But that doesn't mean we shouldn't try.

On one occasion, "*Jesus asked, 'Why do you call me 'Lord' if you don't do what I say?'*" (Luke 6:46) Ouch! That hurts. Is it possible that you misrepresent Christ with a pseudo-Christianity, saying one thing but doing another? We might call ourselves "Christians," but we don't live as loyal followers of Christ. Talk about taking the name of the Lord in vain!

So, how do we live up to the standard? Is it by strictly following a set of rules, such as the Ten Commandments? You know, Jesus wasn't critical of the Pharisees because they kept the rules; He was critical of them because they didn't go any deeper than that. They were content with the outside appearance. Remember when Jesus compared them to cups and bowls that were clean on the outside but filthy inside? Listen to Jesus' instruction on how to fix that. Matthew 23:26 says, "*You blind Pharisee! First wash the inside of the cup and the dish, and then the outside will become clean, too.*"

You need to let God take care of cleaning the inside, and as a result, you will want to clean up the outside. Sometimes people will tell you, "It's what's on the inside that counts." Sure. But I would like to suggest to you that "what's on the inside" is not the only thing that counts. What is on the outside counts too! Let's be honest—regardless of what people say, we always judge a book by its cover. You probably did that with this book!

And I mean, you kind of have to, because you don't have time to read everything! And we do that every day in all kinds of situations, too. We choose which food we are going to eat based on how it looks. If we sell our car, we wash it, wax it, and vacuum it out before we put it up for sale, because it looks nicer. It would be a shame if some people never got to see the inside of you as a Christ-Follower because the outside turned them off.

Unfortunately, sometimes our behavior does. So, if you consider yourself a Christian and if you call yourself a Christ-follower or Disciple of Jesus, then people expect you to follow Him and live like Him.

Jesus said in Matthew 7:17-20, "*A good tree produces good fruit, and a bad tree produces bad fruit. A good tree can't produce bad fruit, and a bad tree can't produce good fruit. So, every tree that does not produce good fruit is chopped down and thrown into the fire.*" Yes, just as you can identify a tree by its fruit, so you can identify people by their actions.

So, what are we to do? That is why the saying goes, "actions speak louder than words." Don't wear masks! Be clean inside *and* outside. Mark Twin said it best: "We're all like the moon; we have a dark side we don't want anyone to see." However, we must be as transparent as possible about our beliefs and actions, so that we don't appear to be claiming one thing while doing something else. The question is, how do we do that?

Paul tells us in Romans 12:2, "*Don't copy the behavior and customs of this world, but let God transform you into a new person by changing the way you think. Then you will learn to know God's will for you, which is good, pleasing, and perfect.*" David said it a little differently in Psalm 51:10, "*Create in me a clean heart, oh God. Renew a loyal spirit within me.*"

It's important to take a step back and get to know yourself. Practice self-awareness. What do your actions and behaviors say about you? What do others think of when they think about you? Are you reflecting Jesus in your life? Do you imitate the qualities of Jesus in your life? By understanding yourself better, you can make more intentional decisions that align with your true identity and purpose.

CHRIST-LIKE QUALITIES

The passage of Philippians 2:3-8 in the opening of this chapter challenges us to examine our attitudes and actions towards others. As

Christian readers, we are called to live a life of humility and service, putting the needs of others above our own. This passage reminds us that true greatness comes from serving others with a selfless heart. Let's be honest, though, sometimes it's difficult to put others' needs before our own. We live in a world that encourages us to look out for number one, to climb the ladder of success at all costs. But as followers of Christ, we are called to a higher standard. We are called to imitate the humble and sacrificial love of our Lord and Savior.

How can you apply this lesson from Philippians to our daily lives? You can start by taking a step back and examining your motives. Are you seeking recognition and praise for your good deeds, or are you serving others out of a genuine desire to show Christ's love? Strive to be more like Jesus, Who humbled Himself and became a servant for our sake. Jesus laid down His life for us, taking on the form of a servant and dying on the cross to save us from our sins. Allow His selfless love to inspire you to live a life of purpose and meaning, putting others' needs before your own. Don't worry, God will always take care of you.

Jesus exemplified certain qualities that we can learn from and apply to our own lives. Foremost, let's talk about Jesus's compassion. Jesus had a heart of gold and was always looking out for those in need. Whether He was healing the sick, feeding the hungry, or simply lending an ear to those who needed it, Jesus showed us the importance of truly caring for others. Remember that golden rule about treating others as you would like to be treated? Well, that's compassion in a nutshell. It is kindness in action.

A true Christian is a kind and understanding person. Paul says to "*be kind to one another*" (Ephesians 4:32) and to "*let your gentleness be known to all men*" (Philippians 4:5). So, text time you see someone struggling, channel your inner Jesus, and show them some love, empathy, and compassion.

Next up, let's discuss Jesus's humility. Humility is all about recognizing our own limitations and putting others before ourselves. So next time you catch yourself boasting about your latest accomplishments, just remember that Jesus wouldn't be bragging about how many followers he has on Instagram.

Despite being the Son of God, Jesus never flaunted His status or demanded special treatment. He was always down to Earth and approachable, making everyone feel welcome in His presence. So, take a page from Jesus's book and remember to stay humble, no matter how successful you become.

A person's office or title does not impress God. In relation to this, the Bible says that the only superior among any of us is the one who serves others. One day, Jesus told the crowd, *"He who exalts himself will be humbled, and he who humbles himself will be exalted"* (Matthew 23:11-12). Paul reminds us that if anyone thinks he is "somebody" he is deceiving himself, for such a thought proves that he is nobody (Galatians 6:3). We are all small people involved in a big job, and only the message we carry makes us great in every sense of the word. So, let us live humbly, and instead point others at Jesus.

Another quality that Jesus exemplified was forgiveness. Jesus forgave His enemies, even as they crucified Him on the cross. Talk about a tough act to follow! But forgiveness is a powerful tool that can bring healing and peace to all parties involved. So, next time someone wrongs you, try to channel your inner Jesus and offer them forgiveness.

Finally, is patience. Ah, patience—the virtue that we all pray for while waiting in line at the grocery store behind that person with forty-seven items in the ten-items-or-less lane. But patience is about learning to trust in God's timing and not getting frustrated when things don't go our way.

So, take a deep breath, count to ten, and remember that even Jesus had to deal with a bunch of disciples who just didn't seem to get it sometimes.

Jesus was the ultimate role model for compassion, humility, forgiveness, and patience. And these are just a few of the Christ-like qualities we should strive to embody as we navigate life and live up to the standard. When Jesus lives in you, you will be patient, kind, forgiving, humble, and cheerful in irritating situations. You will have a gentle heart for others.

By reflecting on how Jesus exemplified these qualities, we can learn valuable lessons that will help us live with purpose and reclaim our stolen identities. So, let's all strive to be a little more like Jesus and spread love, kindness, and forgiveness wherever we go. We are all works in progress, but with a little help from above, we can all become a little more like Jesus every day. And hey, if all else fails, just remember: What Would Jesus Do?

We must connect ourselves to Jesus like a fetus connects to their mother through the umbilical cord. Think of Jesus as the melody in life, and you must make the harmony. But you must be in tune with Him to live in such a way. You must stand up for what is right. Just as Jesus always stood up and spoke up about what was right. What would the world be today if Abraham Lincoln had given up and given in to political pressure? How would the world be today if Martin Luther had recanted? What if the Nazi's—many actually professed to be Christians—would have stood up against Hitler?

Just because you are a certain way ("That's the way I was raised, and that is how I am...") it does not mean that you must stay way. You can always choose a new "you." Don't just be yourself; be the best version of yourself; one that reflects Jesus.

As a true disciple of Jesus, you must have a proper sense of responsibility and purpose in this world. Ephesians 5:15-17 says, "*Be very careful, then, how you live—not as unwise but as wise, making the most of every opportunity, because the days are evil. Therefore, do not be foolish, but understand what the Lord's will is."* And Proverbs 4:24-27 adds, *"Keep your mouth free of perversity; keep corrupt talk far from your lips. Let your eyes look straight ahead; fix your gaze directly before you. Give careful thought to the paths for your feet and be steadfast in all your ways. Do not turn to the right or the left; keep your foot from evil."*

BEING PROSPEROUS

If you truly want to reflect Jesus in life, then you must understand it is not about you. We live in a world that teaches us to always look for number one and to step on anyone that stands in our way to succeed. I've heard a saying that says, "Successful people consistently do what others only do occasionally." It's a great quote. However, I have a fundamental issue with the idea of success.

So, I want to test you on one item. It is in the definition of "Success." Again, it is a good word, and please don't stop using it. But let me knock you off balance for just a moment. I dislike that word. Let me rephrase that. The problem I have with that word is the attitude that we have when we use it. Before judging me, allow me to elaborate. When two teams go to play a game on the field, it means that one will have success over the other one because one will win. But what about the other one?

You see, when you go by that definition and with that attitude of success, those teams go out to the field and, by requirement (the fans fully expect it), one team must succeed over the other one. One must win and one must lose. I don't like that kind of success. In fact, I don't want you to succeed in life if it means that everyone else around you fails. That is not the model of Christ! How can your life be successful if it means that other ones will fail?

Now, what I am about to tell you right now might go against anything and everything you've been thinking of in your life. If that is the case, good. Allow me to shake your foundation. And I won't apologize. I will, however, expand upon it.

Hear me now: do not succeed! That's right. You read that right. Now, you are probably confused. I understand. "*What are you saying? Oh, no, you didn't!*" But you read it right. Do-not-succeed. Instead, follow this Biblical model.

God told Jeremiah, "*I have plans for you. Plans to prosper you, not to harm you.*" So, don't be successful, instead, prosper. Let me tell you the difference between prosperity and success. Oh, and please do me a favor. Do not go out of here and every time you hear the word "success" don't think of it like a curse word. "*Ah, no... Obed told us that that is not a good word to use.*" No! Please do not miss the point here. I am talking about your attitude towards the word "success." In fact, if anything, I want you to think of success in terms of prosperity now. Because when God blesses you and prospers you, everyone around you is blessed!

It is not convenient for you to be successful if you are simply going to get ahead and then forget about others. What have you gained if you do that? What do you gain, if you make it in life—whatever that means for you—and God makes you successful and you make money, and your career is launched, and your business flourishes, but then you forget about other people, your community?

The world needs prosperous people, not merely successful! We need people who will say, "I love my country, I love my church, I love my people, I love my community, I love the place where God allows me to live, I love the school that I came from, I love my family, and I love the people of the world."

If we don't learn to love others besides ourselves and besides those who look and/or think like us, the world is doomed. So, you must be prosperous, not successful, so that everyone around you can share in your joy and be blessed. God did not call us to be successful. There are people starving in this world who need prosperous individuals to remember them.

We need prosperous Christians who go out and make a positive impact on society at large; those who go out and are so blessed by God that when they touch something, it flourishes. Because the Lord says that when you are faithful, anything that your hand touches will flourish.

LET GOD PICK YOUR PATH AND GUIDE YOU

When you look at high school yearbooks, students put what they aspire to be when they grow up. When I was younger, I used to tell people as a joke, *"When I am older, I will be an adult."* But really, under my picture in the yearbook, I think I once put "Rock Star" or something like that. I probably put that because I learned one should do what one enjoys and at what one is at least somewhat good.

But at some point, in my journey, thankfully, God got a hold of me and told me, *"Obed, I have plans for you. Plans to prosper you and not to harm you. My grace is sufficient for you."* I tried to do what I wanted, and it didn't work, and then I surrender and said, *"God, you show me what you want me to do."* Then He showed me the jobs that I was supposed to do.

Now, I've made several career changes in my life. Even at my age, I still wake up many days and don't know what I am supposed to do. But I let God lead and I just follow. Sometimes it changes in nature and in location. Sometimes He really takes me out of my comfort zone. I also have accumulated a lot of students' debt! But God guides my career and takes care of me. And God will guide you too!

If you take your God-given gifts and your skills gained through your education, life experience, and hard work, including those that you will gain in the future, and you go out into the world and live by this principle, God will lead you. You simply must trust God. Give it your best, as it's not in vain. Paul reminds us, "always give yourselves fully to the work of the Lord, because you know that your labor in the Lord is not in vain" (1 Corinthians 15:58).

Let me tell you this: in every position that I have been in, I have never been the most qualified. And hear me now, as hard as it may sound, chances are that you will never be the most qualified for a position, either. There is always someone better than you at something. And that is okay. You know why? Because if God calls you to do something, then He will qualify you for that. Be willing to let go and let God lead, and then do your best, and you will be prosperous.

This applies to your career, to your relationships, and everything else in life. So, you might not be the most qualified person for the job at hand, and in fact, sometimes you might even know what you're doing. But check this out: God, in His mercy, guides you. So, even though you might not be a good person, you still serve a great God. And He is merciful with His servants.

God has a specific plan for you. And you must humbly live within this principle. You must let God guide your life so that you can be prosperous and be useful to humanity. This is what it means simply put: if you are or are planning on becoming a medical doctor, don't get into it for the money; get into it for the patients and to serve others in the ministry of healing. If you are or are going to be a teacher, don't do it for recognition. Do it to inspire new generations to become better people.

Whatever you do or plan to do, do it for the human beings that will seek you for your unique God-given gifts and expertise to live enhanced lives. Remember that you are here to serve this world and fellow humanity. Use best practice in whatever you do. Micah put it better when he said in Micah 5:8, "*Do justice, love mercy, and walk humbly with God.*" That is how you change the world, and that is your purpose.

CHANGE THE WORLD

Go out there and transform the world! Get out there and make it a better place. That's your mission as a disciple of Jesus. Live your purpose out loud. Be a part of the solution! Don't you dare become successful; be prosperous so that everywhere around you is blessed. Be prosperous, so that whatever your hand touches, it flourishes. Do not sit around waiting for someone to take care of you. To rephrase what John F. Kennedy once said, "*Ask not what the world can do for you; ask what you can do for the world.*" Practice the traits of Jesus as you live selflessly. That is how you live up to the standard.

Living up to the standard and being prosperous in life is not about having a great career, an important title, or a fancy office at your work or school. Greatness is when you are among the people in the trenches, making the world a better place. So, be courageous and dare to make a difference. God is calling you right now to change the world, one person at a time.

The question is: Are you listening? Are you willing to risk losing your career and to be misunderstood for a righteous cause, if that is what it takes? Are you willing to trust God in His direction in your life, even when you are not sure of where you are headed? Are you willing to let go of success and humbly be a light for your community? Well, then, make this world a better place, for God has ordained it so.

Keep your chin up; for this battle is not yours, it is God's. He wants to use you. Just be willing. Make this world a place where people will come to know God through medicine, through law, through teaching, through business, through music, through psychology, or through whatever your God-given skill is.

There is power when your degree, education, title, and gifts belong to Jesus. And when your whole life belongs to Him, you can change the world into a better place. Come out of anonymity into history. Do something extraordinary! And as Paul says, "*whatever you do, work at it with all your heart, as working for the Lord, not for human masters*" (Colossians 3:23).

○•●•○

"Dear Jesus, help me reflect Your character by producing good fruit and being prosperous. Amen."

Chapter 11

WHAT WILL YOU BE KNOWN FOR?

"In the same way, let your light shine before others, that they may see your good deeds and glorify your Father in Heaven."

(Matthew 5:16)

LEGACY AND IMPACT

HAVE YOU EVER STOPPED TO THINK about how people will remember you? I mean, when you are gone and folks stop by your grave or sit around in the house and talk about you, what will they say? Will they recall you for the right things? For a righteous lifestyle? Perhaps you're wondering if anyone will even remember you at all.

A young man stood up at a funeral to say a few words about his best friend. "I still can't get over the fact that he is gone. I also can't get over the fact that I totally survived that same car accident! Can you believe it? I should have suffered the same injuries like... like... what's-his-name here?"

As Christians, we must consider the impact we make on those around us. After all, we are called to be the light of the world, not the dim flashlight that gets lost in the junk drawer. Our legacy is like a ripple effect, spreading out into the world and touching the lives of others in ways we may never even realize.

Think about it—would you rather be remembered as the grumpy old man who yelled at kids to get off his lawn, or as the kind-hearted soul who brought joy and laughter wherever they went? The choice is yours. Leaving a positive legacy is not just about being remembered fondly; it's about making a lasting impact on the worlds.

So, again, if you were gone today, would people say that you were great at your job, worked hard and made tons of money? Would they say you were a nice person always helping your neighbor? Perhaps that you were a caring husband, father, mother, or wife.

If we are honest with ourselves, some of us might have to admit that if we died today, we wouldn't leave a very positive memory behind. Maybe we were selfish, never told our children, parents, or spouse that we loved them. Maybe we worked too many hours. Or maybe people might recall us as the type of person who held grudges too easily, or that always wanted to gossip about other people.

I don't believe anyone would consciously say they want to leave this Earth with a bad reputation. Or that they would want people to remember them only for how selfish, troublemaking, rude, or fake they were. Everyone aspires to be remembered for something special. Someone once said, "When you were born, everyone else was smiling and you were crying. Live so that when you die, everyone else is crying and you are smiling."

But let me tell you this: you have a unique opportunity to leave a legacy of love, grace, and compassion. You have a calling and an invitation to be a beacon of light in a world that can often feel dark and hopeless. By living out your purpose with intentionality and authenticity, you can inspire others to do the same. Imagine the ripple effect of positivity that could spread throughout the world if we commit to leaving a positive legacy.

A son sat beside his father's bedside; the father was near death. "Is that you, my son?" the father asked.

"Yes, father; it is I," replied the son.

"What is that smell? Is mother making my favorite apple pie?"

"Yes, father," said the son.

"Ah, to have one more piece before I leave. Would you bring me a piece?" asked the weakened father.

After a few minutes, the son returns and sits down next to his father.

"Is that you, my son?"

"Yes, father."

"Did you bring me the pie?"

"No, dad. Mom said that the pie is for after your funeral!"

Well, this is all a little humorous. However, hopefully, our life will have amounted to a little more than a piece of apple pie.

Interestingly, though, people often remember the bad things you have done. For example, people remember Peter's denial, not his preaching at Pentecost; David's sin with Bathsheba, not bringing the Ark back home; Jonah running from God, not his powerful preaching of repentance at Nineveh; and Eve's sin, as opposed to her beginnings. So, praise God that He forgives us!

What do you wish to be remembered for? What legacy do you want to leave behind? Is it good things or bad? When I ask that question, I am not only asking you how you would like to be remembered after your death, but how you would like to be remembered even now whenever your name comes up.

For the Apostle Paul, this was no idle question. When he wrote the second letter to Timothy, he was in prison, in chains, in Rome, under a sentence of imminent death. He didn't have many days left to live. He did not have five years left and he most likely did not have five months to get his act together. The grains of sand had nearly all slipped from the hourglass. Death by beheading was not far away. Paul knew he would never get out of prison alive. That is why he said, "*I have finished the race.*" For him, the race of life was towards the end. The only thing left was to send a message to his young protégé, Timothy, and give him a last word of encouragement. Then he could face his death with grace and courage.

But think about this! How is Paul remembered today? You know, his life ended at the hands of that sadistic madman, Nero, the exalted emperor of the Roman Empire. Nero was the most powerful man in the world at his time. And who was Paul, really? Just a Jewish preacher who claimed to be a follower of Jesus. A troublemaker, but nothing compared to the mighty Nero. Soon, the emperor would order him put to death. But that was not the end of the story. Two thousand years have passed. What does the world say now about Nero and about Paul? We name our dogs Nero and our sons Paul.

We should remember each other as Paul was remembered. We should love one another in such a way that we also desire to help one another in times of need, and rejoice with those who rejoice, and weep with those who weep. We should desire to be remembered as those who set an example for others to follow, so that when people think of us, they would thank God for letting us have a place in their lives, because we provided a life for them to imitate.

So, how will people think of you once you are gone? What legacy will you leave behind? Build your life on Jesus and love as He loved, unconditionally, and those who know you will be sorry to see you go. I'll tell you this: if when I'm gone, they remember I was a loving and lovable individual who truly believed in Jesus and lived like Him, then I will not have lived in vain. I hope the same goes for you.

And as you consider this, I urge you to reflect on the legacy that you are already building and that you will leave behind. Are you living with purpose and intentionality, or are you simply going through the motions? Remember, you are a divine masterpiece, created with a unique purpose and calling. Embrace your identity, reclaim your stolen purpose, and live it out loud for all to see. Your legacy is waiting to be written—make it a good one.

LIVING INTENTIONALLY

Are you tired of living life on autopilot, just going through the motions day after day? Do you feel you're not making a real impact on the world around you? Well, it's time to shake things up and start living with intentionality! Living with a clear purpose, you can make a lasting impact on those around you.

Living with intentionality means being deliberate in your actions and choices. It means taking the time to think about the impact you want to have on the world and then taking steps to make that impact a reality. It's about being present in the moment and making the most of every opportunity that comes your way. So, put down that remote control and get ready to live with purpose and on purpose.

As Christians, we are called to be salt and light in the world, to make a difference wherever we go. Living with intentionality is a way to fulfill that calling and make a lasting impact on the people around us. Whether it's through acts of kindness, sharing the love of Christ, or simply being a listening ear to someone in need, there are countless ways to make a difference in the world. So, roll up your sleeves and get to work.

Living with intentionality also means being aware of the impact of your words and actions on others. It's about being mindful of how you interact with those around you and striving to always leave a positive impression. So, the next time you're tempted to gossip or say something hurtful, remember to pause and think about the impact of your words. You have the power to build others up or tear them down, so choose wisely!

Living with intentionality is a powerful way to reclaim your stolen identity and live out your purpose as a divine masterpiece. So, commit to being intentional in all that you do, whether it's at work, at home, or in your community. Make a lasting impact on the world around you and show others the love of Christ through your actions. This way, you will make a difference and leave a positive legacy that will last for generations to come.

Do not just be yourself; be the best version of yourself! In everything you do, try your best. Remember, discipleship is a lifestyle, so make daily habits to be a better person. Take advantage of every opportunity to make someone's day better. Opportunities are never lost; someone always takes the ones you missed. So, don't let someone else take on your legacy. There are no second-chance opportunities for first-time impressions. Make the best of each one!

It doesn't take much to make someone's day. Paul and Peter give us good examples to follow. In Romans 12:18, Paul says, "*Do not repay anyone evil for evil. Be careful to do what is right in the eyes of everyone. If it is possible, as far as it depends on you, live at peace with everyone.*" And in 1 Peter 4:8-11, Peter adds, "*Above all, love each other deeply, because love covers a multitude of sins. Offer hospitality to one another without grumbling. Each of you should use whatever gift you have received to serve others, as faithful stewards of God's grace in its various forms. If anyone speaks, they should do so as one who speaks the very words of God. If anyone serves, they should do so with the strength God provides, so that in all things God may be praised through Jesus Christ."* That is how you build a great legacy.

Help others. Smile often. In fact, remember that a smile is an inexpensive way to improve your looks. So, try it today! Unless, of course, your teeth are horrible (like mine). Also, don't hold on to grudges. That is not Christ-like. Do not use your daily energy or time to dwell on who offended you. Do not do yourself or others a disservice! While it is true, you cannot control what other people say about you or do to you, you can still choose how to respond. Do not give them the power to own you by not forgiving and by holding grudges. Do as Jesus would do. I know it's easier said than done, but we can try this daily. Remember, *"don't let the sun go down on your anger"* (Ephesians 4:26).

Taking intentional actions also means preparing. This will allow you to be ready for the unexpected. It also helps to avoid costly mistakes when discipling. When you prepare, you avoid potential issues. You don't want to be like the nervous pastor who got his words twisted on his first day at a new church. He said, "I have come here to heal the dead, cast out the sick, and raise the devil!" So you must reflect, prepare, and act.

REFLECTION AND ACTION

I urge you once again to reflect on the question: What kind of legacy do you want to leave behind? Are you aiming for a legacy of love, kindness, and generosity? Or maybe you desire to be known for your faith, resilience, and unwavering commitment to God. Whatever it may be, take some time to think about the impact you want to have on the world around you. Whatever it is, you must start today.

Consider how you can live out your legacy daily. Are there acts of kindness you can do for others? Can you volunteer at a local charity or lend a listening ear to a friend in need? Remember, even the smallest actions can have a ripple effect and leave a lasting impact on those around you.

Matthew 5:16 reminds us we are called to let our light shine before others, so that they may see our good works and give glory to our Father in Heaven. Like the children's song says, it's time to stop hiding our light under a bushel and let it shine bright like a diamond.

Think of Matthew 5:16 as the ultimate pep talk from Jesus. He's saying, *"Hey you, yes you with the doubts and insecurities, it's time to stop playing small and start living up to your full potential."* So, listen to Him and start living your purpose intentionally. Shine your light so bright even the darkest corners of your life illuminate with love, joy, and hope. Because when you do, you not only bring glory to God but also inspire others to do the same. Be the light in a world that so desperately needs it.

○•●•○

"Dear Jesus, help me live my life with purpose, intentionally making this world a better place, one person at a time. May I leave a positive legacy, as I bring others to You. In Your name I pray, Amen."

Chapter 12

ON BEING GOD'S TEMPLE

"Do you not know that your bodies are temples of the Holy Spirit,
Who is in you, Whom you have received from God? You are not your
own; you were bought at a price. Therefore honor God with your
bodies."

(1 Corinthians 6:19-20)

TEMPLE OF THE HOLY SPIRIT

A DOG-FOOD COMPANY'S NEWEST PRODUCT wasn't selling well. The president called in his management staff. "How's our advertising?" he asked.

"Great," replied the advertising executive. "This ad campaign will probably win the industry's top awards this year."

"All right," the president continued. "How about our product design?"

The production manager spoke up. "It's great boss. Our new label and packaging scored high in every marketing test we ran."

"Hmmm. Well, how's our sales staff? Are they doing their job?"

The sales manager was quick to respond. "Oh, sure. Our people are the best in the business."

There was heavy silence as the president thought about what he had just heard. "We've got great advertising, great packaging, a top-notch sales force, yet this product is coming in dead last in the dog food market. Does anyone have any idea what the problem might be?"

Everyone looked at each other in silence. Finally, one brave soul spoke up. "It's those stupid dogs, sir. They just won't touch the stuff."

Sometimes the church is like that in trying to reach the unchurched, but many times we have this problem also with those that are already Christians. We can have the slickest advertising, the nicest facilities, the best Bible studies, the most wonderful music, but we can't get the people to understand what a wonderful opportunity we have for them. And the problem comes down to what people believe about themselves in relationship to who they are in Jesus. When we understand the promises that are given to us by God as Christians, we will live life to its fullest and take advantage of every opportunity that will aid us in becoming more like Jesus.

In Christ, I am God's Temple—we are the dwelling place of God Almighty. I want to focus on two passages of Scripture—one focuses on the individual being God's Temple, and the other focuses on us, as the Church, being God's Temple.

❖ *"Don't you know that your body is the temple of the Holy Spirit, Who lives in you and was given to you by God? You do not belong to yourself, for God bought you with a high price. So, you must honor God with your body."* (1 Corinthians 6:19-20)

❖ *"Don't you realize that all of you together are the temple of God and that the Spirit of God lives in you? God will bring ruin upon anyone who ruins*

this temple. For God's temple is holy, and you Christians are that temple."
(1 Corinthians 3:16-17)

You see, God lives in everyone in the person of the Holy Spirit. And God lives in His Church as Christians meet corporately, too. God is both in you, and in the place that you gathered with others who also have God dwelling in them. And what we need to understand is that God is not dwelling in you and dwelling in some place of worship in an abstract, symbolic kind of way—God is physically and spiritually here as a present reality as much as we are. Hopefully, this allows you to discover just how special and important you really are!

As Christians, we often hear the phrase "your body is a temple of the Holy Spirit" thrown around. But what does that mean? Well, imagine your body as a fancy mansion, and the Holy Spirit as the VIP guest who gets to live there. You wouldn't want to let your guest down by neglecting your mansion, would you? So, you must take care of yourself, inside and out, because you are a special place for the Holy Spirit to dwell.

Being the temple of the Holy Spirit means you always have a direct line to God. So next time you're feeling down or lost, remember that you have the Holy Spirit living inside you, ready to guide and comfort you through any situation.

But just like any suitable host, it's important to keep your temple clean and free of any distractions that might hinder your connection with the Holy Spirit. So, take some time each day to declutter your mind and heart and make room for God to shine through. It'll be amazing how much brighter your life will be when you allow the Holy Spirit to take the lead.

Embrace your role and purpose as the temple of the Holy Spirit and let your light shine brightly for all to see. Go forth with confidence, knowing that the Holy Spirit is with you every step of the way.

GOD LIVES HERE

In the Old Testament, the Temple was the place God promised to meet His people, Israel. They would come to this physical structure and God would appear to them. It wasn't as if God lived within the four walls of the building, but that He would be present there for the people. *"I have set apart this Temple you have built so that My name will be honored there forever. I will always watch over it and care for it"* (1 Kings 9:3).

God is saying to Solomon, *"I will meet with you here at the temple. This is the place for you to come, for the people to come, and for the world to come. This is the meeting place."* And since Christ has come, God has taken it a giant step further. God says that our heart is the place where He dwells— not temporarily, but He lives here forever. Like the Old Testament temple, God exists in many places at one time, but His presence within us and within His church is real and unending. God literally lives with us every day, every moment, in every situation. *"Don't you realize that all of you together are the temple of God and that the Spirit of God lives in you?"* (1 Corinthians 3:16)

Paul is not talking about God appearing in a cloud, or in the Ark of the Covenant; he is saying that God really lives in each one of us and in His Church. We are the Temple of Almighty God. We are His dwelling place, His habitation. Now, when you understand and accept this truth, you naturally begin examining your life, your attitude, your commitment level, and just about everything else in your life. You will look at these things everywhere you go and everything you do. God is with you and God is *in* you.

When you fully recognize and embrace this, you will be filled with a power unknown to you before—it is a realization that God loves you, that

God fills you with His power, that God gives you the ability to do what He asks you to do, and that God enables you to live your life to the fullest.

As I write this, I can see a baseball glove here. The glove can't do anything by itself, but when my hand is in it, it can do many things. True, it isn't the glove, but my hand in the glove that acts. We are gloves—it is the Holy Spirit inside us Who is the hand and does the job. Now, what we must do is make room for the hand, so every finger is filled.

God lives in you, but He will only become fully operative in your life when you are ready for Him to fill you and use you to do His work. Ephesians gives us two texts along these lines—one applies to us as individuals, and the second applies to the Church as a whole:

❖ *"Don't be drunk with wine because that will ruin your life. Instead, let the Holy Spirit fill and control you"* (Ephesians 5:18).

❖ *"The church is His body; it is filled by Christ, Who fills everything everywhere with His presence"* (Ephesians 1:23).

God lives in us and in our church—it is up to us to allow Him to take control. We do that by simply getting ourselves and our agendas out of the way and letting Him take over—He will do it, and we will all benefit from it—and the sooner we do it, the better off we will all be.

GOD IS WORSHIPED HERE

The Temple in the Old Testament was a place to worship God. These psalms speak about it:

❖ *"Because of your unfailing love, I can enter Your house; with deepest awe I will worship at Your Temple"* (Psalms 5:7).

❖ *"Oh God, we meditate on your unfailing love as we worship in Your Temple"* (Psalms 48:9).

❖ *"I bow before Your holy Temple as I worship. I will give thanks to Your name for Your unfailing love and faithfulness because Your promises are backed by all the honor of Your name"* (Psalms 138:2).

The focus in the Old Testament was on going to a place where people could meet and worship God. But now, Paul tells us, we are God's house of worship—both as individuals and as a church. The place where we are at is the place that God is worshiped. God is here, right in your midst. And if you are the Temple of God, and we are the Temple of God collectively, then we must choose to be a Temple filled with worship. Anything less than this is a denial of God's presence among us.

We are God's Temple—we are the place of worship—we have been born again by the Spirit of God to worship God and everything else that we do, say, or think is secondary to that fact. Being a disciple of Jesus starts with a heart of worship; being a biblical scholar starts with a heart of worship; being a gifted musician starts with a heart of worship. Everything that we do as individuals and as a church begins, ends, and subsists on worship, because we are the Temple of God.

GOD IS HONORED HERE

Read the verse from the beginning of the chapter once again, but this time, I want to give you a little background information. The church in Corinth that Paul was writing to had many very serious problems. One problem they were having dealt with people engaging in inappropriate sexual activity that was outside the will of God.

In response, Paul wrote, *"Don't you know that your body is the temple of the Holy Spirit, Who lives in you and was given to you by God? You do not belong to yourself, for God bought you with a high price. So, you must honor God with your body."* (1 Corinthians 6:19-20) He is saying, "How dare you defile the Temple of God which is your body! Don't you realize God is with you in the very midst of your sin?"

The context of the second verse had to do with the church—there were people trying to cause divisions within the church, stirring up controversy, trying to ruin the work that God was doing there. Paul responded by saying, *"Don't you realize that all of you together are the temple of God and that the Spirit of God lives in you? God will bring ruin upon anyone who ruins this temple. For God's temple is holy, and you Christians are that temple."* (1 Corinthians 3:16-17) He is saying, "How dare you try to destroy this Temple that God has constructed with His own hands. How dare you dishonor God by dividing His people?"

In both cases that we've looked at, God's Temple was dishonored when His people engaged in sinful behavior, either by themselves or as a group. What we need to understand is we, as the Temple of God, bring God with us everywhere that we go. Every time we lie, God is there. Every time that we watch a movie, God is there. Every time that we go to work, God is there. Every time that we go to church, God is there. And when we go to these places or engage in various activities, we need to understand that we are literally including God in all of them.

So, what we want to make sure is that the things that we say and do, and the places that we go, are going to bring honor to God rather than dishonor. *"Do not bring sorrow to God's Holy Spirit by the way you live. Remember, He is the One Who has identified you as His own, guaranteeing that you will be saved on the day of redemption"* (Ephesians 4:30).

Since you now know God lives in you, what will you attempt for Him you were afraid to attempt before? Since you now know God wants your worship, what needs to change to make Him in your life? Since you now know that God wants you to honor Him, how will you live differently from this day forward?

IMPLICATIONS

Since we know our bodies are temples of the Holy Spirit, it is evidently important to take care of them. That means eating right, exercising regularly, and getting enough sleep. As Christians, we must also strive to live a life of integrity and honesty. But let's be honest, sometimes it's hard to resist the urge to tell a little white lie or gossip about that annoying coworker. So, here's a tip: before you open your mouth, ask yourself, what would Jesus do? And if you can't imagine Jesus spreading rumors or cheating on His taxes, then maybe you should think twice before doing it yourself.

Maintaining your physical, mental, and spiritual health will have a direct impact on your character. So, remember to take care of your entire self, strive to be a person of integrity, and nurture your relationships with love and kindness. Approach life holistically. Holistic living is not just about eating organic kale and doing yoga in your living room; it's about nurturing your entire being—spiritually, physically, and emotionally. As Christians, we believe we are fearfully and wonderfully made by God, so it only makes sense to take care of ourselves holistically.

Spiritually, holistic living means seeking God in all areas of our lives. It's not just about going to church on the weekends, but about having a personal relationship with Him every day. When we are healthy in spirit, we are more at peace, more joyful, and more connected to the source of all life.

Physically, holistic living involves taking care of our bodies as temples of the Holy Spirit. This means eating well, exercising, and getting appropriate rest. And emotionally, holistic living is all about dealing with our feelings healthily. This might mean talking to a therapist, journaling, or just having a good, cathartic cry occasionally. It's important to acknowledge our emotions and work through them so we can be emotionally stable and resilient.

For anything to endure, it needs to have a solid foundation, just like in a building. So make sure you are building a good foundation in your body. If you want to live a long, healthy life, make sure you are mindful of what you eat and drink. If you want to have a fit mindset, make sure you are purposefully putting good things in your mind and consuming things that edify. Strive for holistic living in all areas of your life. Seek God in everything you do, take care of your body as temples of the Holy Spirit.

The thought of my body being a temple is both awe-inspiring and slightly intimidating. I mean, I love a good Netflix binge and ice cream as much as the next person, but when I remember that the Holy Spirit is chilling out in my temple, I suddenly feel the need to do some major spring cleaning. Out with junk food, in with kale smoothies!

The next time that you're feeling a little down about your appearance or struggling with self-doubt, just remember that you are a temple of the Holy Spirit, created by God Himself. Embrace your unique quirks and imperfections and remember that your purpose in life goes far beyond what you see in the mirror. You are loved, cherished, have a purpose, and you are valued beyond measure. You are the dwelling place of God, a masterpiece; live accordingly!

o•●•o

"Dear Jesus, thank You for allowing me to be the dwelling place of the Holy Spirit. Help me live in such a way that honors His presence in my life.
Amen."

Chapter 13

A NEW CREATION

"Therefore, if anyone is in Christ, the new creation has come: The old has gone, the new is here!"

(2 Corinthians 5:17)

TRANSFORMATION IN CHRIST

ARE YOU TIRED OF FEELING LIKE A BLAND, old potato when you know you were born a glorious, sparkling diamond? In this chapter, we are diving deep into the transformative power of being a new creation in Christ. So, say goodbye to your old self, and hello to a brand new, shiny version of yourself! Remember that a pearl goes through a process of great suffering. Hang in there.

When you accept Christ into your life, you are not just signing up for a onetime makeover. You are embarking on a lifelong journey of transformation. Just like a caterpillar turning into a beautiful butterfly, you are shedding your old ways and stepping into the fullness of who God created you to be.

We can find the perfect example of this transformation in the story of Mephiboshet found in 2 Samuel. By the time of this story, there had been many battles, but the war was finally over. The Philistines had killed both Saul and his son, Jonathan. David, by now, was the new king. In those days, the new king often killed all the remaining family members of the previous king, so there would be no further competition for the throne. Although David had no intention of doing this, Saul's family was fearful and hurried to escape, taking with them Jonathan's son, Mephibosheth.

In that time, Saul's lineage had practically been extinguished with the death of Ish-Boshet, his son, who was Jonathan's brother. He was the strong one, the best suited to be the next king (2 Samuel 2:8-30). Mephiboshet was now the only candidate left alive from Saul's lineage to take over the throne.

2 Samuel 4:4 says that Mephibosheth was only five years old when the Philistines killed his father, Jonathan, and grandfather Saul in battle. On that day, everyone in his home panicked. The Philistines were ruthless and would surely try to kill Saul's entire household. Meanwhile, David and his guerilla troops were wandering around. Saul's descendants were terrified that if the Philistines didn't get them, David surely would.

They all knew about the problems that had arisen between David and Saul years earlier. So, they grabbed what they could and fled. When the nurse grabbed Mephibosheth and fled with him, she tripped and the young boy fell, breaking both his ankles. The ankles didn't recover correctly, and Mephibosheth was crippled for the rest of his life.

Years later, David called a man named Ziba into his presence. Ziba had been the chief steward of Saul's house. David asked Ziba if there was anyone left who was a descendent of Saul's. Ziba said, "*Well, the only person left is a crippled guy who is the son of Jonathan.*" Maybe Ziba meant, "*Don't worry. There's only a crippled man who couldn't be a threat to you.*"

If a king was trying to establish a new dynasty, it was typical for him to worry about this. If there was anyone left from the previous dynasty, that person could always claim to be the rightful heir to the throne. But David wasn't worried about that. He was worried about his covenant with Jonathan (2 Samuel 21:7).

In 1 Samuel 18:3 and 20:15-17, the following is recorded: "*And Jonathan made a covenant with David because he loved him as himself.*" "*'Do not ever cut off your kindness from my family—not even when the Lord has cut off every one of David's enemies from the face of the earth.' So, Jonathan made a covenant with the house of David, saying, "May the Lord call David's enemies to account." And Jonathan had David reaffirm his oath out of love for him, because he loved him as he loved himself.*"

David and Jonathan had been such close friends that they promised that if anything happened to each other, the other would take care of their children. So, David asked Ziba, several times, "*Is there anyone remaining in the house of Saul to whom I may show kindness?*" Now, you must understand the meaning of the word for kindness in the original Hebrew. It is *hessed.* It involves both love and obligation. It also refers to the tender love we have received from God.

"*Is there anyone,*" David wants to know, "*to whom I can be as kind and lovingly committed as God has been to me?*" Ziba answered, "*Just a cripple.*" But all that David wanted to know next was "*Where is he?*" (verse 4) He didn't ask, "*How badly crippled?*" or "*How did it happen?*" Just, "*Where is he?*" That is the only question that God wants to know about you as well. "*Where are you?*" He is not asking, "*What happened to you?*" or "*Who is to blame for your problems?*" Just, "*Where are you?*"

Ziba didn't even use Mephibosheth's name. He just called him the lame son of Jonathan, as if the disability defined him. And he told David that Mephibosheth was in a place called Lo-Debar, which means: "a place where there is no pasture." It was east of the Jordan River (2 Samuel 17:27-29).

That is always where we end up when we are defined by our weaknesses—in the infertile, unfruitful place. It was commonly believed in those times that where there was no pasture, there was no peace. Jerusalem means of "City of Peace."

Mephibosheth was crippled, both physically and emotionally. For some of us, the weakness is a physical disability; They cannot walk or see or hear or think clearly. However, for most of us, the disability is spiritual. We struggle with self-esteem and other problems such as this. Many times, it is because long ago we got hurt and remain crippled by it. Perhaps we were hurt by a member of the church, but whatever the reason, we all have some kind of weakness or disability. And Romans 3:23 also reminds us we have all been crippled by the fall of sin.

It doesn't matter how successful you become in Lo-Debar (that infertile, unfruitful place), you know that if you allow yourself to be identified by your problem, life will still feel so unproductive. That is why we must ignore our weaknesses and identify ourselves with our strengths. Remember that God only asks, as David did, *"Where are you?"* That is because He wants neither to classify you by your weakness nor define you by your problems. All He wants is to find you and bring you back home to the palace where you belong. He wants to take you to His royal table. We have lived in exile in an unfruitful place of sin for too long! And the King wants to bring us home to eat at His table and restore us as princes and princesses.

Imagine how many years Mephibosheth lived in fear of the day he would hear that knock on his door! Then one day, the royal messenger came saying King David wanted to see him. And he didn't have a choice.

Mephibosheth must have thought that this was his end. King David would surely feel threatened by Saul's grandson and want to kill him.

Can you see the misery of this picture when Mephibosheth appeared in David's presence? He limped into the throne room, face down with fear and shame, and when he saw King David, the crutches went flying as this disabled man fell on his face in front of the man he had always feared. That's what the Bible says (verse 6)! Mephibosheth thought David was going to give him what he deserved according to the custom of those times. However, to Mephibosheth's surprise, King David said, *"Do not be afraid."*

It is amazing how many times that sentence appears in the Bible... *"Do not be afraid."* When God, the King of Heaven, sent His angelic messengers to find those living in infertile places, they always began by saying, *"Fear not! I bring you good news."* While Mephibosheth lay on the ground expecting David's sword to fall on his neck, he heard, *"Fear not, I will show you kindness, tender hessed, for the sake of your father, Jonathan."* You see, not for Mephibosheth's sake, but for the sake of his father!

David doesn't just use words, but also actions, as you must when you are expressing love. The Bible story says that David restored all of Saul's land to Mephibosheth; so now he not only had forgiveness but also income. David also gave him a place at his own royal table; so now he had honor. He adopted Mephibosheth, making him, as the text says, *"like one of the king's own sons."* You see, from there on, David saw Mephibosheth not just as a cripple guy, the grandchild of his enemy, but as one of his own children—a prince!

Mephiboshet means "shame." "I am a dead dog," he had said. And that is exactly how he considered himself against David (2 Samuel 9:8). We too, like Mephibosheth, have all fallen. Some of us fell into evil habits, or damaging illusions about life, but all of us have fallen into sin. As a result, we are all crippled, dog-like, and unable to walk out of the place where life has taken us. That's why the gospel focuses on God's pursuit of us through Jesus. When He finds us, He gives us His loving grace and loving *hessed.* He restores us. He gives us a place at His table. He adopts us into the King's family as princes and princesses (vs. 7, 10-11, and 13).

Four times this passage of 2 Samuel 9 says, *"You will always eat at my table."* And he did; it was at the table of the King that Mephiboshet found healing. We, too, can find healing in God's table. We are all equal there. Everybody looks the same height sitting at a table—it doesn't matter your handicaps.

The census tells us that there are over eighty million people live in this country with physical or mental disabilities; but there are over eight billion people, including you and me, who have spiritual disabilities—that's all of us. And like Mephibosheth, we have all fallen or have been dropped into something, and the hurts just stay with us the rest of our life. In our weakness, we know we need a Savior.

However, in Luke 14:15-24, Jesus describes His kingdom as a banquet hall filled with *"the poor, the crippled, the blind, and the lame."* Why? Because these are the people who know they need a Savior. You must also know if you need a Savior.

You see, the story of Mephibosheth is a story of grace, where a king reaches down to someone in trouble. King David changed a fugitive into a prince; the Savior changes us from disabled into beloved—from fugitives into His sons and daughters. A new identity in Him! That's grace. It is God giving us what we don't deserve. That is *hessed...* that is forgiveness... that is restoration... and that is love!

Now, the question is, have you accepted the invitation? He has called you out of that unfruitful place into Jerusalem, the city of peace. Romans 5:1 says, *"Therefore, since we have been declared righteous by faith, we have peace with God through our Lord Jesus Christ, through Whom we have also obtained access by faith into this grace in which we stand, and we rejoice in the hope of God's glory."*

When we come to God through a new birth by faith in Christ, He gives us a new nature, a new heart, a new life, a new hope, a new identity, and a new purpose. He restores us to His own image. He takes us, ordinary people, and makes us extraordinary. He makes us new creations. That is why 1 Corinthians 5:17 says, *"So then, if anyone is in Christ, he is a new creation; what is old has passed away, what is new has come!"* How refreshing is that?

It's like a spiritual makeover, but without the hefty price tag or the risk of a bad haircut. Imagine being able to hit the reset button on your life and start fresh, all thanks to Jesus! No more carrying around the baggage of your past mistakes or letting your insecurities define you. You are a new creation, my friend, a divine masterpiece in the making.

Do you want to join Him at His table? Do you want to receive from Him this mew identity of royalty? Do you want to be a new creation in Him?

LIVING AS A NEW CREATION

Being a new creation in Christ is not just a onetime event, it's a lifelong process of growth and transformation. And living as a new creation can be a real challenge, especially when you're used to living as an old, crusty creation. But we can embrace our new identity with God's help.

Foremost, it's important to remember that you are a new creation in Christ. That means no more living in the past or dwelling on your past mistakes. It's time to let go of that old identity and embrace the new one that God has given you. So, next time you catch yourself feeling down about your past, just remember that you are a new creation, a masterpiece created in God's image and destined for greatness, with a sit on the King's table.

One way to live out your new identity daily is by surrounding yourself with positive influences. Whether it's through reading uplifting books, listening to inspiring music, or spending time with encouraging friends, make sure you're filling your mind and heart with positivity. After all, you can't expect to live as a new creation if you're constantly surrounded by negativity.

Another important aspect of living as a new creation is to practice gratitude. Take time each day to thank God for all that He has done for you and all that He will continue to do. Gratitude not only helps you to appreciate the blessings in your life, but it also helps you to stay focused on the positive aspects of your new identity. Remember, you changed when you trusted Christ. Your very spiritual DNA was rewritten, and you became a new person. The change happened right away. Be eternally grateful for that.

Sometimes it is more convenient to stay blind, crippled, etc., because of sin. But Jesus calls us to stand up, see, walk, and share His good news! Being a new creation means we must live accordingly. You must remind yourself daily who you are now. A new life has begun. Live it joyfully!

You are righteous because of Christ. All the guilt, shame, and sin that used to define you are no longer true. That old life is gone. A new life has begun. All the accusations that Satan hurls your way are no longer true about you. You can confidently say as Paul said, *"I have been crucified with Christ and I no longer live, but Christ lives in me. The life I now live in the body, I live by faith in the Son of God, Who loved me and gave Himself for me"* (Galatians 2:20).

Even after Mephiboshet was brought to the king's palace, he continued to face challenges. Some people questioned his presence. The same will be with you as a new creation. Challenges are a part of life, and as Christians, we are not exempt from facing them. Sometimes it can feel like we are facing more challenges than ever before. Whether personal struggles, financial difficulties, or health issues, there are always obstacles standing in our way. Just remember that God is always by your side, ready to help you overcome any challenge that comes your way. And just like David stood up for Mephiboshet, Jesus stands up for you.

Another challenge we may face is feeling like you are not living up to our full potential. It's easy to compare yourselves to others and feel you are falling short. But remember that God has a unique plan and purpose for you. The standards of this world do not define your identity. Embrace who you are in Him and the gifts that He has given you, and trust that He will guide you on the path to fulfilling your purpose.

As you face life's challenges, know that you are not alone. God is with you every step of the way, guiding you, strengthening you, and encouraging you. And the next time you dwell on your shortcomings or feeling like you're not good enough, just remember 1 Corinthians 5:17. You are not who you used to be—you are a brand-new creation. Let that truth sink deep into your soul and remind you of who you truly are in Christ.

○•●•○

"Dear Jesus, thank You for making me a new creation and giving me a place at your table. Thank You for lifting me up to the status of royalty. Help me reflect on my new identity in You. In Jesus' name, Amen."

Chapter 14

REJOICE IN THE LORD ALWAYS

"Rejoice in the Lord always. I will say it again: Rejoice!"

(Philippians 4:4)

UNDER THE INFLUENCE OF THE SPIRIT

IMAGINE THE HAPPIEST DAY IN YOUR LIFE. Perhaps it was when your parents finally took you to Disneyland as a kid. Maybe it was when you finally afforded that car you really wanted, or when you graduated from college. Mine were when my son and my daughter were born. Even though they were long and uncertain days, becoming a father was one of the best things that ever happened to me.

Happiness is the one thing all people seek. One person seeks it in one way, and another seeks it in another way. Some seek money because they think that money will make them happy. Others seek worldly pleasure because they think that worldly pleasure will make them happy. Others seek learning, the knowledge of science, philosophy, history, or literature, because they think that learning brings genuine joy; but we are all in pursuit of this same thing.

That is why we try to marry the person of our dreams. That is why we go to college. That is why we work hard in life. But you do not need to have anything external or material in order to be happy. Some say that you can simply choose to be happy, however, it doesn't work that way. And that is also why many who seek happiness tirelessly do not find it.

But there is a way, a simple, yet sure way that is open to all, not only to find happiness, but to be truly happy. Listen to what Peter says, "*Though you have not seen Him, you love Him; and even though you do not see Him now, you believe in Him and are filled with an inexpressible (indescribable) and glorious joy*" (1 Peter 1:8). I like it even better in the version of The Message Bible. It says, "*You've never seen Him, yet you love Him. You still don't see Him, yet you trust Him—with laughter and singing, with gladness and happiness.*"

Many people believe you can only gain happiness with material things. If something is not a tangible and visible item, then it will not make you happy. But they are mistaken! This verse lets us know that anyone who really believes in Jesus rejoices with an "inexpressible and glorious joy." Everyone who really believes in Him rejoices with a jubilant joy that is beyond description. And those who do truly believe in Jesus are the only ones who rejoice this way.

Others may have a certain amount of happiness, a certain measure of gladness, but the only people who really know "inexpressible and glorious joy" are those who really believe in Jesus, those who find their identity and purpose in Him. Many people are only happy when things are happening the way they want, but there's a saying that says that when everything is coming your way, you might be in the wrong lane!

Interestingly, many people in society see Christians as miserable people—individuals who have no sense of humor and no joy in life. I've heard some say that we don't know how to laugh or how to have fun. But they are wrong! In fact, the happiest people I know are the most Christ-like people I know.

A group of my friends from the ministry group I was involved with while at college and I were coming back home from a spiritual retreat up in the mountains, and we stopped at a gas station. We were jumping and singing, shouting and laughing as hard as we could. We were having, as one would say, "too much fun." Some people there started looking at us as if we were crazy or as if we were on something. Apparently, it seemed unusual for those watching us that a bunch of young people would be as happy as we were. Perhaps they thought we had drunk a ton of coffee, and the effect was coming out.

A young man approached me and suspiciously asked me, "Hey, bro, what substance are you guys on?" I stared at him and realized that he thought we were all high! So, I told him, "Man, we are on the good one. We are all under the influence of some good stuff that if you had it too, you would be flying! This one sets you free big time. We are under the influence of the Holy Spirit." This led to a great conversation about true joy with him and we ministered to him at that moment.

INEXPRESSIBLE AND GLORIOUS JOY ORIGINS

Let me tell you why those who believe in and have a personal relationship with Jesus live happier lives. First, they have an "inexpressible and glorious joy" because they know their sins are forgiven. Psalms 32:1 says, *"There is no happiness like the joy of knowing your sins are all forgiven."*

What joy fills the heart when someone knows that their sins are fully, freely, and forever forgiven? That is one reason someone who believes in Jesus is joyful. In all other major religions, the followers strive to rid themselves of sin through various practices. They may pray in a prescribed way, do various works, deny themselves legitimate pleasures, follow strict restrictions, lie on beds of nails, go into solitude, etc. However, that is not the case with Jesus. Jesus shows His uniqueness through His statement, "*The Son of Man has power on Earth to forgive sins*" (Matthew 9:6). No other religious leader has ever made this claim! That is a big difference.

Those who believe in Jesus rejoice with "inexpressible and glorious joy" because they know for certain that they will live forever. Isn't that something to rejoice over? We read in 1 John 2:17, "*The world and its desires pass away, but the man who does the will of God lives forever.*" We all know that it is true, as this same verse says, "*the world passes away.*" We certainly ought to know it by this time; but it is equally true "*he who does the will of God lives forever.*"

Paul understood this very well. Over and over in Philippians, he tells us to rejoice in the Lord (see Philippians 2:18; 3:1; 4:4). Paul said this to the Philippians when he was in prison in Rome. Similarly, when Paul and Silas were in prison in Philippi (Acts 16), they were singing praises to God in the night. When Peter and John returned to the Christians of Jerusalem, after being persecuted by the Sanhedrin, the congregation joined in praising God (Acts 4:24-30).

And those who truly believe in Jesus and surrender absolutely to Him, rejoice with "inexpressible and glorious joy" because God gives them the Holy Spirit, and there is no other joy in the present life like the joy of the Holy Spirit.

Since we Christians have received so much forgiveness, the gift of salvation, the promise of living in Heaven, having God's presence through the Holy Spirit, and endless blessings daily, we should therefore be happy! To be a Christian means to be filled with joy. Because what is there not to be happy about? Besides, Christians should be happy also for a testimony to others.

Unfortunately, many times we behave like chameleons, changing colors when changing the environment. Sometimes we are joyful Christians, and the next day we are all "decaffeinated" Christians, without joy or energy. And I'm not saying that we need coffee to be happy, but that since we have already received so much, we should therefore be joyful.

The song we all grew up singing says: "Rejoice in the Lord *always*, and again I say, Rejoice!" It does not say "sometimes," it says "always." That is what we must do—rejoice for we have "the good stuff." We have Jesus in our hearts! If you are in need, remember what Jesus said in Matthew 6:25-34:

"Therefore, I tell you, do not worry about your life, what you will eat or drink; or about your body, what you will wear. Isn't life more than food, and the body more than clothes? Look at the birds of the air; they do not sow or reap or store away in barns, and yet your heavenly Father feeds them. Are you not much more valuable than they are? Can any one of you by worrying add a single hour to your life? And why do you worry about clothes? See how the flowers of the field grow. They do not labor or spin. Yet I tell you that not even Solomon in all his splendor, was dressed like one of these. If that is how God clothes the grass of the field, which is here today and tomorrow is thrown into the fire, will he not much more clothe you—you of little faith? So, do not worry, saying, 'What shall we eat?' or 'What shall we drink?' or 'What shall we wear?' For the pagans run after all these things, and your heavenly Father knows that you need them. But seek first His kingdom and His righteousness, and all these things will be given to you as well. Therefore, do not worry about tomorrow, for tomorrow will worry about itself. Each day has enough trouble of its own."

Jesus says, "Don't worry, be happy. I'm taking care of you." And if you are miserable or unhappy simply because of the way you were born (not cute, thin, or thick enough), just try being born again. So, either way, rejoice always!

In your own joy, make this a great day for someone else. It'll bring you even more joy as well. Every time you smile, sadness disappears and hope is illuminated. And if you meet someone who is feeling down, remind them that God didn't promise days without pain, laughter without sorrow, or sun without rain, but He did promise strength for the day, comfort for the tears, and light for the way. He promised to turn our mourning into dancing and our sorrows into joy!

Even if your own days are gloomy, cheer! The sun will soon come back! And guess what? The Son will also come back soon! So, let us rejoice in Him.

○•●•○

"Dear Jesus, thank You for being the source of joy in my life. Allow me to keep You in my heart and radiate Your joy so that others can come to know you as well. Amen."

PART THREE

Full Circle

Chapter 15

IT'S ALL ABOUT HIM

"So, whether you eat or drink or whatever you do, do it all for the glory of God."

(1 Corinthians 10:31)

DON'T FOCUS ON SELF, FOCUS ON JESUS

HAVE YOU EVER HAD ONE OF THOSE DAYS** where you just can't seem to remember who or where you are? Maybe you put your keys in the fridge or called your boss "mom" by accident. We've all been there. Life can be chaotic. From spilled coffee to missed deadlines, it's easy to get overwhelmed and lose sight of who we are and why we're here. But remember, if there is anything you've learned so far, it's that you can only find your true identity and purpose in one place: Jesus.

It's easy to get caught up in the hustle and bustle of everyday life, but when you take a moment to focus on God, you are reminded that your identity is not found in your job title or social media followers. Your identity is found in Him alone. When you focus on God, you are reminded that He is in control. When you focus on God, you are reminded that you are His beloved child, fearfully and wonderfully made in His image. And your identity and purpose ultimately point back to God because He is the One Who designed you with a specific plan and purpose in mind. Your identity and purpose are not determined by the world around you, but by the God Who created you. As you see, our identity and purpose ultimately always point back to God.

However, when discussing anything, we must always start at the beginning and end at the end. It sounds so simple and maybe even obvious; but many times, we don't do that. Thankfully, the Bible is clear that God is the Alpha and the Omega—the beginning and the end. This means that in everything we do, we must start and end with Christ. After all, Jesus is our Savior, our Teacher, our Example, and our Hope. So we must focus on Him, not on self.

Jesus is the embodiment of God's love, offering salvation through His sacrifice on the cross. By focusing on Him, we find redemption and eternal life. Through His parables and teachings, Jesus provides wisdom and guidance for our daily lives. His words challenge and inspire us to live according to God's will. Jesus' life serves as the perfect model of love, compassion, and obedience to God. By emulating His actions, we grow in our faith and impact the world around us. And as we focus on Jesus, we find hope for the future. His promises of eternal life and His second coming give us strength to persevere through life's challenges.

As Christians, it's also essential to understand our history and origins. While many begin and trace our origins in the first century, I believe we must go back even further. The earliest record of Christian history comes in Genesis 1. The supremacy and authority of Jesus are clear in the Creation story. When He commanded, "Let there be light," the response was immediate—there was light. The Creation story both begins and ends with His voice.

Creation occurred because it recognized and obeyed the supremacy of the Creator, the source of everything. His Word introduced the incredible creative process that brought us into existence. This is the earliest recorded history of the Church. "*Then God blessed them, and God said to them, 'Be fruitful and multiply; fill the Earth...'*" (Genesis 1:28), and here we are today.

John described God's coming into the world by stating, "The Word," the same Word through Whom we were made, "*became One of us.*" John 1 introduces Jesus as "the Word" (or Logos in Greek), emphasizing His eternal existence with God before Creation. This profound concept reveals Jesus' divine nature and pre-existence. John says that "*Through Him all things were made,*" highlighting Jesus' role in the creation of the universe. This connects Him directly to the Genesis account and affirms His deity.

"*The Word became flesh and made His dwelling among us*" beautifully expresses the miracle of the incarnation. God, in the person of Jesus, entered human history to reveal Himself to us. And then, this Logos, or Word, Jesus with us, then began to call us. To the first disciples He said, "Come," and He says to us today, "Come, follow Me." And that is how the church came to be.

Interestingly, the term "Christian" was created as a mocking title to those first century followers of Jesus (Acts 11:26; 26:28). However, and much to the disappointment of those who enjoyed using the designation to sneer at them, the title was quickly adopted as a badge of honor by those early followers of Jesus.

But because He became One with us, we can consider ourselves one with Him and we can dare to call ourselves His followers, His servants, His friends, His brothers, and sisters, and His sons and daughters, His disciples. We can take the name of Christ and call ourselves Christians.

And in that name, we have hope, we have salvation, and we have victory. But most importantly, it is in that name that we find our true identity and purpose.

Jesus does not call us to follow a religion, denomination, congregation, preacher, cause, or movement. He calls us to Himself. Matthew 4:19-21 says, " *'Come, follow Me,' Jesus said, 'and I will make you fishers of men.' At once they left their nets and followed Him. Going on from there, He saw two other brothers, James, son of Zebedee, and his brother John. They were in a boat with their father, Zebedee, repairing their nets. Jesus called them, and immediately they left the boat and their father and followed Him.* " Jesus' call is an invitation to a transformative journey. It's not just about belief, but about actively following in His footsteps and embracing His teachings in our daily life.

The disciples' immediate response, leaving their nets and boats behind, demonstrates the power of Jesus' call. It challenges us to consider what we might need to leave behind to fully follow Christ. Jesus promises to make them "fishers of men," giving their lives new meaning and purpose. This call extends to all believers, inviting us to participate in God's mission of drawing others to Him.

JESUS: FULLY GOD & FULLY HUMAN

The doctrine of the person of Christ is a foundational teaching of Christianity and was the focus of the first three centuries of church history. The creeds of the church affirm that Jesus Christ is fully human and fully God. In humanity, He was born of Mary; in His Divine nature, He was conceived by the Holy Spirit. In His emotions, as a human, He experience joy, sorrow, and anger; in His Divine nature He was perfect in love and compassion. As a human He grew in wisdom; as Divinity, He is all-knowing. He became tired and hunger, and yet he performed miracles. As a human He died on a cross; as God, He rose from the dead.

Jesus is a Divine mediator: He uniquely bridges the gap between God and humanity. As both fully God and fully human, He initiates and maintains our relationship with the Father. He is the supreme authority, the fulfillment of Scripture, and the embodiment of the good news.

John presents Him as the eternal Word, Who was with the Father from all eternity and is the "*only begotten Son*" (John 1:14) of the Father. Jesus is the Creator (John 1:3; Colossians 1:16). Paul tells us, "*For in Him all the fullness of Deity dwells in bodily form, and in Him you have been made complete, and He is the head over all rule and authority*" (Colossians 2:9-10).

Religion is humanity's search for God, but Christianity is different; it is God's search for humanity. I have heard people say, "I found the Lord ten years ago", as though God had been lost. However, God was not lost; we were. And He started the search for us, and not the other way around. He reached out first! He searched for you and said, "Come."

There is a unique relationship between God and humanity, and Jesus introduced it. Christ took on human flesh and became One with us. Born of a human woman, He identified with our humanity. Born in a stable, He identified with our poverty. Born of an unwed mother, He identified with our humiliation. Tempted in the desert, He identified with our struggles. Rejected by those He came to save, He identified with our alienation. Crucified on a cross, He took the punishment for our sins. Buried in a borrowed grave, He identified with our mortality. Rising from the dead, He gave us hope of eternal life. And ascended into Heaven, He has prepared a place for us to live with Him as a family.

Jesus knew His identity and He was never swayed from it, even in suffering an undeserved and brutal death on our behalf. Even as He was tempted to question His identity and even as He was mocked and condemned to death for saying who He really was, His solid sense of identity allowed Him to endure. He overcame death and came back to life to restore our relationship with God, enjoying spiritual life, securing our identity as His children and renewing our purpose to know Him as our heavenly Father.

You see, our theology as Christians makes so much sense with Jesus, and very little sense without Him. It's not just in the name, but in the Person from Whom the name derives. The Christian gospel is not simply forgiveness of sins, as many Christians believe—it is rather the sharing of God's life—the Alpha and Omega. The Gospel is the good news of Jesus, Immanuel—God amongst us! For Christianity, the Gospel and Truth are not something we know; it is Someone we follow.

The Bible reveals Jesus on every page. In fact, the Bible's purpose is not spiritual enrichment or moral counsel, but the "Word of God," which is Jesus—God with us. Jesus told His disciples in John 5:39, "*The Scriptures testify of Me.*" The New Testament is all about Jesus; and the Old Testament is the promise and the passing of the seed of Jesus through the history of humanity. And because of this, Christ must be the center of everything.

ALL AUTHORITY IS HIS

Without Jesus, there is no message, there is no gospel, and there is no past, present, or future. It is not about His teachings, but about Him as a Person. He is the Creator, and we are the created. He is the Head, and we are the body. We must be careful not to minimize or summarize Jesus to just a one paragraph of our fundamental beliefs. He must be the central gospel. And we must center all other teachings and beliefs on Jesus! Christians worship a living God. We do not worship a dead philosopher. His tomb is empty! And even now, He reigns supreme.

In fact, Jesus claims, not most of the authority, but *all* authority. This includes comprehensive authority extending over all creation, spiritual realms, and human affairs. In Matthew, Jesus says, *"My Father has given Me authority over everything. No one really knows the Son except the Father, and no one really knows the Father except the Son and those to whom the Son chooses to reveal Him"* (Matthew 11:27).

Now, it's important to delve into this statement. These words of Jesus warrant deliberate thought. *"My Father has given Me authority over everything."* This has big implications, because Jesus is claiming unshared supremacy. This is a unique relationship. Jesus speaks of the intimate, exclusive relationship between Himself and the Father. This divine connection underscores His authority and ability to reveal the Father to us. He is the One Who chooses to reveal the Father. This emphasizes His role as the sole mediator between God and humanity, guiding us into a deeper understanding of the divine.

The author of Hebrews says, *"He sustains everything by the mighty power of His command"* (Hebrews 1:3). You see, Jesus claims to be, not a top theologian or a prophet of God (as some religions claim He is), but God Himself. The Author of life. Heaven's door has one key, and Jesus holds it.

OUR PURPOSE: LIVING FOR GOD'S GLORY

The Christian faith is all about Jesus Christ. And it should come as no shock or surprise that our entire lives, including our identities and purpose, must be linked to Him. We exist for a purpose, which is to bring Him glory. So, you must live with the purpose of glorifying God.

Living for His glory means living with intent to bring honor and praise to Him in everything you do. It means waking up each day with the mindset that you exist to fulfill a greater purpose than just going through the motions. When you live for His glory, you see the world through a different lens. Suddenly, the little things that used to bother you don't seem so important anymore.

1 Corinthians 10:31 is a reminder that we should do everything for the glory of God. And that means everything—from the way we work, to the way we interact with others, everything we do can be an opportunity to bring Him glory. In all aspects of our lives, whether it's what we eat, how we work, or how we treat others, you must try to bring Him honor and glory.

Our lives must be Christ-centered, not ego-centered. This is why Paul said, "*This is the truth I have known, Jesus Christ crucified and resurrected*" (1 Corinthians 2:2). There is no true existence apart from Him. It is not about you. God does not need your title, your talents, your money, or time. It is about Him!

So, you do not need to know your "self-worth" and "self-identity" so much as you need to know Christ. To know Who He is and to know Him as your Lord and Savior are much more important than any self-worth and self-identity. Many people get discouraged because they only focus on their present circumstances or in trying to find out who they are apart from God. But you must set your eyes on Jesus!

It is in Jesus that you have a new identity, and it is *that* identity that must predominate. It is upon *that* identity that you must stand. In Christ, by new birth and by adoption, you are now a child of God. And as you affirm and reaffirm who you are in Christ, you will discover a change in your thinking, your feelings, and your behavior as you seek to personify and exemplify what it means to be in Christ. So, don't cheat on Jesus; be faithfully committed and live in a relationship with Him.

This invitation to a relationship with Him, which promises a solid identity and purpose, is free to every person who accepts it. Jesus said, "*Behold I stand at the door and knock, if anyone hears My voice and opens the door, I will come in to him and dine with Him and he with Me"* (Revelation 3:20). This statement is an analogy of an ongoing invitation for everyone to have a relationship with Him. This relationship is what we are all longing and searching for because we were created for it. And without a relationship with Jesus, we will not find our true identity or purpose.

THE CENTER

Have you ever noticed how everyone always wants to be at the center of everything? We all aspire to be in the middle of something. And that is because it is in the center where things happen. It is where the excitement is. For example:

❖ Sitting in the middle of the theater watching a movie, as opposed to the side view.

❖ Walking down the center aisle for a wedding, as opposed to a side aisle of some kind. It would be weird otherwise.

❖ The middle of a tootsie roll pop. How many licks does it take to get to the center of a Tootsie Roll?

❖ The middle of most Mexican candy. The spicy part is the best!

❖ The center of the stadium or arena, getting as close as you can to the game, for a better view.

❖ The heart of a good fruit, since it is usually the sweetest part.

❖ Even throughout human history, this has been the case. Since the beginning of our time, everyone has wanted to know what is at the center of the universe. Before, most people used to believe that the Earth was the center of the universe. (You see, humans have been self-centered for a lengthy time.)

To make room, we usually tell people to move towards the middle, or *center*. Whenever the church is full, and there are people standing, we make an announcement to move to the center of the aisles to make room for others so they can join us. In the same way, to make room in your life, you must also move to the center—where Jesus is.

Move to the center? What does that mean? I will elaborate on that. But the first question I must ask you today is: What is at the center of *your* life? Is Jesus in the center of your life? I ask you this because, as I already mentioned, we are self-centered people. We need to become Christ-centered individuals, because if Jesus is at the center of your life, He will be lifted, and people will automatically be drawn unto Him. But if your life is not automatically drawing people to Him, then you must question whether He is at the center of your life. This means you are not living out your purpose as intended.

Unfortunately, the bride, the Church, which is made of individuals, is more focused on herself than on the Groom, Jesus. Like in Nazareth, we might have Jesus, but still miss Christ. You might be familiar with Him to the point of missing His true identity. Proximity breeds familiarity. There is a positive and a negative side to that. We must be careful not to make Jesus so mundane that we take Him for granted.

Even when Jesus asked His disciples, *"Who do people say I am?"* They replied with four different answers (Matthew 16:13-16). When Jesus walked on Earth, people were confused as to His true identity. Some thought He was a prophet, others a great political leader, still others thought He was John the Baptist come back to life. Who do *you* say He is? This is important, because not knowing Who He is will mean that we put ourselves or something else at the center of our lives.

When we put Jesus at the center of our lives, there is a paradigm shift. There is cognitive reconstruction in how we perceive things regarding worldviews. We no longer think of things the same way. Our perceptions and our politics change: we no longer think about matters of left versus right. What matters is if it is Christ-centered or not. Being in the center does not mean compromising in a *middle* ground that is balanced. In here, the center does not mean middle, as in a compromise. It means allowing Jesus to take us wherever He leads.

One concept that helps grasp this idea is the difference between bounded versus centered sets. A bounded set is where we create a boundary, a theological border, a doctrinal fence, and separate those who are inside the fence from those who are out. It is an "us" versus "them" mentality where everyone on the inside is accepted, loved, and welcomed, while those outside the fence are kept away until they can change their beliefs and behaviors to fit the entry requirements.

Think of a bounded set as a Western-style horse corral. The cowboys build the fence to keep the horses from wandering away. Outside the fence is where wild beasts dwell, just looking for a chance to kill a horse. In this situation, the fence serves to protect the property of the cowboys, and makes it easier for them to feed and care for their herd. Occasionally, a wild animal gets into the corral, where it is shot.

Sometimes, however, the cowboys go out and capture some mustangs from the wild and bring them back to the corral. But before these wild horses can be introduced to the rest of the herd, they must be broken. They must learn to enjoy the safety of the fence.

Usually, the wild horses are tamed, and introduced to the rest of the herd. Though they may still long for the freedom of the open range, they eventually learn that life inside the corral is pretty good. There are no predators, and the food is easy to get. It is safe, warm, and clean, and there is plenty of time for food and friendship with other horses. One can easily see the many similarities between the image of the horse corral and what is today the most prominent model for church. Doctrinal statements and membership requirements serve as the fence.

But here is a different model I propose to you as a better approach. It is a centered set. In a centered set, there are no boundaries. There are no walls. There is no fence. There is no dividing line between "us" and "them," no rules or guidelines to determine who is "in" and who is "out." Everyone is loved, welcomed, and accepted, no matter what. Everyone automatically "belongs."

But how does it work? Isn't that chaos, you might ask? How is this different from just a random mass of people wandering around? The answer is: because of what is at the center. A centered set has no boundaries to keep people out, but it has something so compelling at the center that pulls people in. There are no gatekeepers turning people away, for everyone is being pulled toward the center.

While everyone "belongs" in the set, involvement in the set is not based on who has made it through the gate and is now inside the fence, but it is based on the proximity to the center, and the direction in which they are moving. Those who are closest to the center, who cluster around the center, will be the most involved with each other, for they will also be closer to each other. Those who are further out, but who are also moving toward the center, may also be involved with each other as they are drawn in. But they are not looked down upon for being "further out," for everyone else, at some point or another, were also further out of the center.

Everybody recognizes it takes time to be drawn in, and some move faster, and others move slower. Some even move backwards. Some get closer to the center, but dislike what they see, so they head back in the opposite direction. Everybody understands this because everybody has done it. But no matter how far someone pulls back, at no point do they ever stop "belonging" for there is no outer boundary that can be crossed. There is plenty of room for everyone.

If a horse corral helped picture the bounded set, a water hole in the African grasslands might be a good picture of a centered set. There will be only one watering hole for miles and miles in any direction. This means that animals that live in the area will never stray too far from the water, especially in the dry season.

During the rainy season, they may stray further from the hole, but they always know where the water can be found, just in case the rains do not come. And during the dry season, when the rains do not come and the grass withers away and the ground is parched, it is common to find hundreds of different animals all sharing the same watering hole.

Animals that at any other time of year might stay away from each other, or even prey on one another, will live in relative peace and safety near the water hole. Lions, zebras, deer, and birds will drink from the same water. And while the rains are absent, they will not stray too far from the water, for they know that this water hole is their life. There are no fences to pen them in, and no cowboys to keep the peace, and yet the draw of the water is enough to accomplish both.

You see, by putting Jesus at the center, where He belongs, and by us moving towards the center, people of all backgrounds and beliefs will be welcomed at the table to join in the conversation, to serve the community, to learn from and challenge each other, and to encourage one another to move ever closer to Jesus. In such an atmosphere, there is room for people of all faiths, all backgrounds, all races, and all creeds. This also means recognizing that the best way to present the gospel irresistibly is to show Jesus, as He *is* the Gospel!

Christianity must be a Christ-centered entity. In a centered-set church, it is recognized that we are all sinners, all struggling to be the best people we can be. But we also believe that the closer one gets to the center, which is Jesus, the more Christlike one's behavior should become. No one is unworthy of belonging. This way, there is plenty of room for everyone. But we help each other come closer to each other by coming closer to Jesus at the center of it all.

My prayer and my challenge for you today is for you to become a Christ-centered individual. Only by being centered in the Alpha and the Omega will you find peace. Only by putting your trust in the Creator will you find comfort. Only by allowing Him to direct your life will you find your true identity and purpose. After all, it really is all about Him!

Remember that nothing can separate you from Jesus—not death, not life, not angels or demons, not even the past, the present, or future, no height or depth, nothing! He is always with you to help you and guide you. He will never leave you nor forsake you. You should never leave Him either! He will always guide you and you should always follow Him. He will always sustain you, and you should always trust Him.

OH CAPTAIN, MY CAPTAIN

I'd like to share a personal story that reflects His guiding presence in our lives. I used to work as a dean at a university for a decade, and each year, we would take about one-hundred students up to Yosemite National Park for a wonderful camp during the Winter, where we would meet students from another two Christian universities. We called it Tri-Campus Retreat. Every year, we would get snow since it was in January, and each time it was a wonderful experience.

Every year, I would take a group of students on different hikes. Some years we did easy hikes, and in other years we would do some of the most difficult ones in the park. The group that would come with me each year varied in size and personalities, and this also determined which hike we would go on. At times, there were some repeat students that would come each year. Now, I've always enjoyed the great outdoors, but hiking with several energetic college students on snow and ice can be a whole different ball game.

Well, this one time, we packed our bags, loaded up on snacks, and set off on what was supposed to be a simple, refreshing hike to one of the big falls. As we were hiking, one of my crazy but fun male students, being the adventurous spirit he was, ran ahead. "I'm going to be the leader!" he declared, charging up the trail. Two girls in the group, not wanting to be outdone, quickly followed him. Those remaining and I tried to keep up, but we were soon left behind, walking at a more leisurely pace, enjoying the scenery and some rare quiet time in the forest.

About halfway through the hike, we reached a fork in the trail. There were two paths: one that looked well-trodden and another that was less so. Naturally, this student, the "leader," chose the path less traveled. I had a momentary flash wisdom thinking this might be a great teaching moment. Little did I know just how memorable it would become.

We followed the student leader down the trail, and it quickly became plain that this path was not the easy route. It was steep, rocky, and clearly not maintained. To make matters worse, the ground was frozen, and patches of black ice made each step treacherous. Before we knew it, we were scrambling over boulders and ducking under low-hanging branches. This student, still leading, was, of course, loving it. Some of the other students, however, struggled. There was one young lady, about 4'8" and 85 lbs., who struggled that most. We could all see her little legs just couldn't keep up with the rough terrain.

At one point, this crazy male student showed off his rock-climbing skills on what he called "Mount Everest." It was, in fact, just a moderately sized boulder, but I guess to him, it was the tallest peak on Earth. Evidently wanting to impress the girls in the group, he got to the top, struck a triumphant pose, and promptly slipped, landing in a heap at the bottom.

Luckily, there was no harm done—just a bruised ego and a lot of laughter from the rest of us.

But it was around this point that I truly began to worry. This was getting dangerous. I was in charge of this group of college students, and I was the only adult staff. What if something serious happened? What if someone got hurt? What if we couldn't find our way back? By this point we had completely gotten out of course, and there wasn't even a path to follow.

So, we took a break to reassess our situation. As we sat there, catching our breath, I could see the faces in the group as they all worried. Well, most of them. The infamous young man was having the time of his life. But we had no phone signal, and not one of us was entirely sure how to get back to the main trail. And being honest, in that moment, a wave of fear and helplessness washed over me. Of course, I didn't want to scare the group, but I asked them if we could take a moment to pray. We prayed as a group, asking God for guidance and protection.

Then, out of nowhere, I remembered something my father used to say when we got lost on family trips: "When in doubt, find a landmark." I looked around and, through the gaps in the tall trees, I caught a tiny glimpse of El Capitan in the distance, that iconic, massive rock formation in the center of Yosemite National Park.

If you are not familiar with Yosemite, let me tell you about El Capitan. El Capitan is a colossal, immovable guidepost in the park, drawing visitors from all over the world to admire its grandeur and challenge its heights. There have been many documentaries on people trying to climb it. Many have died trying. It is huge and beautiful. **Being its size, the elevated rock formation is usually visible from most parts of the national park. Especially to those who are looking for it!**

And at that moment, for us, it was a beacon of hope in our moment of uncertainty. With renewed determination, I led the group of students back towards it, hoping it would guide us back to the main trail. **And as a sailor seeks land, we grasped towards the rock. Here, it was literally the rock of our salvation.**

As we trudged along, we encountered some wild animals. At one point, we saw a family of black bears, a mom and two young cubs, very close to us. Thankfully, they were minding their own business. We also saw a bunch of types of hoofed mammals, deer and elk, several with huge antlers crossing our path. The presence of these animals reminded us of the dangers lurking around us, and we became even more cautious.

My dear student leader, ever the optimist, tried to convince us he could tame the bears with a granola bar. You see, on the way up, I had done something that you are not supposed to do. While still on the path, I took out some nuts and put them in my hand, and several squirrels came to me and ate out of my hand. (Please don't do as I did when you're out in the wild.) Well, now he wanted to try that with the bear cubs. And I don't think mama bear would've liked that too much. So, of course, we kindly declined his idea and kept moving.

Thankfully, the ground slowly showed a path, and this path slowly began to widen and become more manageable. After what felt like days of being lost in the freezing cold, but was probably just a few hours, we finally emerged back onto a trail. We were tired, hungry, thirsty, dirty, and scratched up, but we were safe.

Later that night, back in the lodge, as we sat around the chimney, the fearless male student leader proudly declared, "See, I told you I could lead us!" The petite girl, with her usual sass, replied, "Yeah, but Dean O (that's how they called me) had to save us!" We all burst into laughter, the tension of the day melting away into the warmth of the fire.

At that moment, I realized something profound. Just like El Capitan guided us back to the main trail, Jesus is always there, guiding us back to the right path when we wander off. He is our Captain! He is *El Capitan...* that is the Captain of captains. And no matter how lost we may feel, He is always there, unmoved, leading and protecting us.

If you are lost in life, do what I did in that forest. Seek Him out. Lift your eyes and set your sights on Jesus, our constant guide and compass. Just as El Capitan stood tall and unwavering right at the center of the national park, guiding us through the wilderness, Jesus stands as the unchanging Captain in the center of our lives too, always ready to lead us back to safety and to the right path of life on which we belong.

WILL YOU ANSWER HIS CALL?

He's calling you to trust Him. Jesus is here with open arms, ready to embrace you, forgive you, and lead you into a life of purpose and joy. Will you surrender your life to Him today? Will you trust Him with your burdens, your worries, your future, and your life? If you're ready to make that decision, I invite you to prayer just where you are and surrender all to Him. Let this be the moment you say, "It's all about You, Jesus." Will you answer His call?

○•●•○

"Dear Jesus, help me deny myself and surrender it all to You. Remind me it is not about me, but about You. May I find my identity and purpose in You alone. Amen."

Conclusion

YOUR IDENTITY, YOUR
PURPOSE, AND YOUR JOURNEY

DEAR READER, as you go on with life, never forget that the opinions of others or the mistakes of your past do not define your identity. You are a divine masterpiece, created by God with a unique purpose and calling. Embrace who you are and walk confidently in the path that God has set before you.

Your purpose is not something to be feared or avoided, but something to be embraced and pursued with passion. God has a plan for your life that is greater than you could ever imagine. Do not be afraid to step out of faith and live your purpose with confidence and boldness. In daily life, bring Him honor and glory by living for Him and by making Him your center.

Your journey may be filled with struggles, twists, and turns, but remember, He is always by your side, guiding you every step of the way. Trust in His plan for your life and know that He has equipped you with everything you need to fulfill your purpose and live a life that brings glory to His name. Go out and live as the beloved child of God, as the prince or princess, and heir to God's Kingdom, that you are.

ACKNOWLEDGMENTS

To all my readers, I want to take a moment to express my deepest gratitude for your support and encouragement. Thank you for picking up this book and embarking on the journey of reclaiming your stolen identities and living out your purpose. May you find inspiration, hope, and a good laugh or two within these pages. Remember that you are a Divine Masterpiece, fearfully and wonderfully made by the Creator of the universe. Embrace your true identity and live it out loud for all the world to see.

To my family and friends who have stood by me through thick and thin, I am eternally grateful for your unwavering love and support. Your words of encouragement and prayers have been the fuel that kept me going when the going got tough. Your unwavering faith and dedication to this process have truly inspired me to keep pushing forward, even when the road seemed long and bumpy. You are all truly gems in the treasure trove of God's creation, and I am blessed to have each and every one of you in my life.

And of course, thanks to the Almighty Himself for guiding me through this writing process. Your divine intervention and gentle nudges in the right direction have been the driving force behind every word on these pages. Without Your grace and mercy, this book would not be possible. I am eternally thankful.

ABOUT THE AUTHOR

Obed Olivarría was born in Mexicali, Mexico and spent his youth as a bicultural transnational citizen. He has a passion for writing both fiction and nonfiction, public speaking, composing, arranging, and performing music, as well as traveling around the world. He loves the thrill of adrenaline-pumping activities, but also the quiet reflection acquired from writing and creating.

Obed has worked as a youth and young adult pastor, as a freelance graphic designer, session musician, ministry consultant, and university dean. Having worked at every level of the education system from pre-k to university has given him an expedition to the human psyche. He has a dynamic love of life and ministry, and is a deep thinker concerning the Gospel of Jesus.

Obed lives in sunny Orange County, California with his charming wife and two energetic children, where he works as a school psychologist by day. In the future, Obed hopes to continue to write inspiring books that entertain, but also challenge the status quo. On a personal level, he would like to visit every country in the world, perhaps drawing inspiration from these travels for another great story.